Endors

Circular Leadership – Together We Rise highlights the transformations that can occur when individual perspectives are shared from the heart with a collective intention and supported by a collaborative circle. Based on participants' insights and experiences, it offers hope for a new way of being and leading that can change the world.

— *Peter Russell, www.peterrussell.com* Author *The Global Brain* and *From Science to God*

Circular Leadership demonstrates the impact of what is possible when people with different backgrounds and belief systems come together in coherence and harmony with a common intention to be of service to humanity. This is a beautiful and powerful book. It provides a way to break the fear-based model of power over people to a new love-based paradigm of power with people. I highly recommend each person on the path to read this anthology and feel the frequency of the intention set by Linda Roebuck and other co-authors. Hats off to Linda Roebuck, for her leadership and spiritual wisdom in providing this work.

— *James Tyberonn, www.Earth-Keeper.com Author, Channel & Founder of Earth-Keeper*

Having been privileged to sit in on a CCC meeting, I'm excited to confirm that *Circular Leadership* is the way of the future, the process clearly outlined in this easy-to-read book. The fact that, unlike linear or hierarchal leadership models, the contributions of every member are respected and appreciated makes this approach new and refreshing. Ultimately, this type of leadership not only leads to consensual decisions and group accountability but also to spiraling growth for all concerned.

— *Christine Page MD www.christinepage.com*
Author, Frontiers of Health

Fascinating, informative, inspiring. *Circular Leadership - Together We Rise* brings a rich and beautiful story of an evolved style of leadership that serves a higher purpose. Author Linda Roebuck and her team of co-creators share ways to transform individually and collectively. This is big. Listen with your Heart. Read with the eyes of your soul. Together we build a positive world.

— *Dr. Katherine E. Johnson, Leadership Coach,*
University Faculty, Reiki Master, Spiritual Guide

Circular Leadership – Together We Rise brings an essential transformation from our linear and hierarchal models to the stability and coherence of the circle, reclaiming the "whole," and offering innovation, expression and heightened sensitivity to all.

Since the circle represents the very foundation of our life, focus on the essence and structure of the circle creates a container formed from each one present. This circular structure brings safety and cohesion in ways that are then grounded in more productivity, clearer communication and stronger group connection, congruence and trust. Throughout their writings, co-authors of this anthology demonstrate this concept of interconnectedness and the grand possibility of a world where when one succeeds, all succeed.

— *Flo Aeveia Magdalena,*
Author of Sunlight on Water:
A Guide to Soul-full Living

Circular Leadership - Together We Rise is an inspirational and empowering book that teaches us how to show up fully in our role at work, home and in organizations where we participate. Circular Leadership provides a roadmap for leadership in the 21st century. It is time that we step up and make a difference in the world. Circular Leadership shows us how to do this together. Step into the circle and offer your fullest potential!

—*Dawn Fleming, www.energytransformations.org,*
Director, Energy Transformations

The ideas in this book take us from an old paradigm of Power Over People to a new love-based paradigm of Power With People and are important to the cultural shifts taking place on the planet.

—Ginny Robertson, Founder On Purpose Woman Community/On Purpose Woman Magazine

In this book, we discover that a new paradigm for organizational leadership is emerging, based upon Trust, Respect, Honesty and Vulnerability. The leadership council of A Community of Transformation, based in Annapolis, MD, has been using this model since its inception. All nineteen contributors have, at one time or another, been part of the leadership council of this organization and share their personal stories of how they have been positively impacted by their participation in this model of circular leadership. I highly recommend this book for anyone or organization seeking to understand the dynamics involved in changing from a hierarchical model of leadership to a circular based one.

—Dr. Kenneth Harris, Synchronicity-The Magic - The Mystery-The Meaning

As evidenced by this book, *Circular Leadership – Together We Rise*, when people form a collective on behalf of the greater good remarkable things happen. This is especially true when the group invites and honors the wisdom of each individual. In this time of profound transformation, individuals and groups alike are being called to serve a higher purpose – a conscious, authentic, love and light filled life. Heart-centered communities practicing Circular Leadership bring forth the gifts of individuals and strengthen the collective by creating fertile ground for transformation and inspiring commitment to the greater, global good.

> — *Teresa Downs Shattuck, PhD, Eco-Therapist, Co-Founder Three Otters Eco Retreat, www.threeotters.com*

CIRCULAR LEADERSHIP
Together We Rise

Copyright © 2019, Linda Roebuck

Published by:
Capucia, LLC
211 Pauline Drive #513
York, PA 17402
www.capuciapublishing.com

ISBN: 978-1-945252-69-3
Library of Congress Control Number: 2019915324

Cover Design & Interior Graphics: Gail McClain
Layout: Ranilo Cabo
Editor and Proofreader: Simon Whaley
Author Photo: Lauren Mudrock
Book Midwife: Carrie Jareed

Printed in the United States of America

CIRCULAR LEADERSHIP
Together We Rise

compiled by
Linda Roebuck
Founder, A Community of Transformation, Inc.

Contents

Introduction

Thank you for choosing to engage with this book. It contains secrets of an evolved style of leadership, one that is circular in nature, steeped in the mysteries of what indigenous peoples and ancient cultures knew. If you're interested in breaking the fear-based model of *power over* people to create a new love-based paradigm of *power with* people, then this book could be what you have been waiting for.

I invite you to read *Circular Leadership: Together We Rise* in a different way than you normally read a book. Take a moment to peruse the table of contents. Turn to a chapter title that speaks to you and read that first. It's a way of shaking things up a bit to move from linear reading and thinking to a circular way of taking in information. Be aware of the writer's intention by letting your heart take in the meaning ... rather than using your head to comprehend the words.

Allow yourself to *feel* the energy offered by these experienced leaders and messengers through the words written on each page. To give you an idea of what I mean, think about the concept of trust. You can define trust, read about trust, discuss how to create trust, etc., but until trust is experienced in relationship with your understanding of a higher consciousness, with self and with others, it cannot be fully known. Awareness of trust is recognized in the individual energetic field and heart space.

Personal trust builds within an individual, and joins with others in sacred circle that are vibrating at a similar frequency. The result is what appears to be a miracle. An energetic field is created within and around the entire group and the space becomes a safe container for each member to be vulnerable, open, and authentic. When this depth of connection, resonance and safety is present, the result is that people are willing to take risks and stretch boundaries together. This is the basis upon which Circular Leadership is built.

As you may already be sensing, the Circular Leadership model is not based on traditional methods of learning and teaching. It is not limited to intellectual or academic knowledge. Circular Leadership must be experienced and felt in order to be understood and known. It requires understanding of, and attention to, the universal principles that apply to all life, expansion and evolution.

Think about that for a moment. What if *leadership* is something deeply rooted in universal truths, energy, vibration, sacredness, authenticity and trust? Just imagine what would be possible for you, your work, and our political and corporate structures if this model of collaboration and co-creation were used across the board! We've used the Circular Leadership style to write this book for you. Each contributor shares learning and discoveries that validate the various components of this transformational model of leadership, thus empowering you to begin to assimilate the aspects of this model in your own life, work, community, etc.

The experiences described in this book come from people with different backgrounds and belief systems. They are written in different styles, and convey different types of content for different purposes. Some of the chapters share personal experiences, some share personal perspectives, and some provide practical guidance. This is intentional. It is reflective of the Circular Leadership model being discussed in that each individual author wrote from the heart on a topic that they were passionate about, in a manner that suited them best. All the authors held the shared intention for the book – to create a work that showcased the personal value and global potential of a model that has been used successfully for almost two decades to operate and manage A Community of Transformation (ACT).

While there are obvious differences among the contributions, there are important similarities across the contributors. Every author has participated with the governing board, or Co-Creation Council (CCC), of ACT. They consider that participation to have had a profound effect on them personally, and the membership as a whole. They consider their time engaging with the CCC as having had a positive impact, and they consider the organization to be successful at its mission.

One important characteristic of every contributor is that they realize their personal inner transformation expands and enhances transformation of the entire group. They are fully aware of the impact their presence has on the totality of the group, whether or not they say anything. They *know* what it means to collaborate and cooperate – to be part of a greater whole.

As you read our chapters, you'll discover the emergence of several themes throughout the book. For example, circle members agree that how we are together is more important than what we do. It is about relationships. In this cooperative and collaborative model, one member's success is everyone's success. And this is what we want to share with you. The grand possibility of a world where we all succeed when one succeeds. No competition. No jealousy. No judgment. No selfishness. But rather a true celebration of each success knowing that someone else's success is ultimately your success too… because we are all interconnected.

In this interconnected world, we have chosen to come together in this way at this time to serve you. It is our collective purpose to share the message of Circular Leadership - a message and model that offers hope for a new way of being and leading that can indeed change the world.

We are delighted you're here to receive this message. And, we thank you for being someone who believes in the possibility of change and transformation on both a personal and global scale.

A new world and a new era are upon us. It starts with you and your circle. The time is now! So, let's begin.

Together We Rise

Music & Lyrics by Bob Sima

I first heard the phrase, "Together We Rise", from Rabia Hayek, a dear friend and mentor. It so moved me, the power of those three words, and I knew it would be a song someday. As Music Coordinator for A Community of Transformation (ACT), and a member of the community, I was both a participant and recipient of the powerful magic of the Circular Leadership.

When Linda Roebuck invited me to participate in the book project, I instantly wanted to be part of it. Admittedly, as time passed I had some procrastination, or call it writer's block, because no ideas were coming for a song. If an idea doesn't hit me immediately, then songs don't get started, or often don't get finished. I sat with the feeling, and I sat and sat. One evening, not long before the manuscript was due, after some worry and concern that nothing had come forth, I was wondering if I was just going to let the opportunity to be part of the project pass me by. That evening, I received a timely, gentle and loving nudge from the Universe (aka Linda). Her message, saying that she felt called to reach out and ask me one more time, no pressure, all in love, just made my heart explode with inspiration. That was just what I needed. I sat in silence and felt the soul of ACT. The line from Rabia came forth and the spark was lit. The song wrote itself that night. I can honestly say that this one was a collaborative effort. The energetics of the ACT tribe, the leadership of Linda Roebuck and a powerful phrase from an old friend, co-wrote this song.

If you want to go fast, then go alone.
If you want to go far you better bring somebody
    else along.

In the moment of darkness, in the moment of truth,
You'll thank your lucky stars that there's someone
    there with you.

There's a beauty in numbers that's impossible to
    deny.
It takes two hands to applaud and a pair of wings
    to reach the sky.

Where there was one, there will be many.
Where there was nothing, there will be plenty.
When me turns to we like the roots from the tree,
It pushes everything up from underneath.

Together we rise, together we thrive.
We believe in circles 'cause circles take no sides.
Together we win when everyone is in.
When every little hand and every little heart,
Touches every little piece and every little part, now.

If you want to start a revolution,
        reach out your hand.
Then lift up a brother or sister and feel the power
        at your command.
If you hold a vision, show everyone what you see.
And watch the tribe come alive to turn your dream
        to reality.

Where there was one, there will be many.
Where there was nothing, there will be plenty.
When me turns to we like the roots from the tree,
It pushes everything up from underneath.

Together we rise, together we thrive.
We believe in circles 'cause circles take no sides.
Together we win when everyone is in.
When every little hand and every little heart,
Touches every little piece and every little part.

What's inside of you is inside of me.
It's amplified when turned into we.
You'll never hear one hand clapping,
Or fly with one wing flapping.

Many hands and many hearts make things happen.
The reason they call it unity is 'cause it all begins
with you and me.

If you want to go fast then go alone.
If you want to go far you better bring somebody
else along.

Together we rise, together we thrive.
We believe in circles 'cause circles take no sides .
Together we win when everyone is in.
When every little hand and every little heart,
Touches every little piece and every little part.

Together we rise, together we thrive.
We believe in circles 'cause circles take no sides.

© Bob Sima Music 2019

Bob Sima

Bob Sima is a troubadour, a way-shower, a guide, an awakener, and a musical mystic. Through the medium of melody and message, he leads listeners to an expanded consciousness, deeper sense of connection, and inner peace and purpose. His music bridges daily life and soul consciousness: the eternal with the now. He delivers instantly accessible songs that take up residence and resonance in your soul. More at www.bobsima.com

Download

Together We Rise

http://bit.ly/CircLead

SCAN ME

Prologue

The Vision and The First Call
—*Linda Roebuck*

Where did all these people come from? I stood in awe, watching as more and more people entered the meeting room of the local library. Flashes of the profound vision I had had a little over two years prior filled me. I clearly remembered being in a highly elevated state of consciousness after participating in a new moon ceremony. This happened on a sacred site with a strong, energetic field. I had been on this hallowed ground before. Each time I had been moved by the sense I was getting of my true Self and what is mine to do. This time was no different.

Earlier that morning, after our ritual, I had decided to walk around the land before leaving for home. The land overlooks a stunning mountain range. As I gazed across the hills and the fields in front of me, all of my senses were heightened. A slight breeze was blowing, and I could smell fresh scents coming from the evergreen trees that lined the edge of the property. I felt the warmth of the sun on my face and wet dew on my feet. The serene setting enhanced a deep state of peace and reverence.

Suddenly the ground started to tremble and shake. I felt as if I was in the middle of an earthquake and I couldn't tell where I ended and the earth began. At that instant my whole body began to vibrate at an accelerated pace, awakening me to a vision of a beautiful, ephemeral rainbow arching across the sky. I saw the words *International Healing and Ascension Center* written in gold and sparkling letters. The vision lasted only a few minutes, during which time my physical body seemed to have been transported to another place and time.

It would be two years before I fully understood the message of the vision. I had almost dismissed the epiphany. Although initially I ignored or doubted the vision I had received, I shifted to a place of becoming more open and curious. The meaning of the word *ascension* was particularly puzzling to me. The inner work I was doing accelerated as I spent more time in meditation, silence, and self-reflection.

An *Aha!* came one day. I understood that ascension was about raising consciousness or awareness. It was about energy, frequency and vibration. My purpose was clear: I was to assist humanity in raising consciousness.

The Call

The Universe had been trying to get my attention over the past few years but I had written off each previous contact as an interesting encounter or phenomenon. This time I could no longer ignore the nudging from my Inner Guidance. I put out a call to the local community. With support of friends, I handed out flyers and placed an ad in the local newspaper that announced a public meeting for people interested in co-creating a multi-purpose center focused on holistic health, spiritual well-being, and peace.

Now, here I was, standing in our local library, welcoming the large crowd who had answered The Call. Overwhelming emotions of gratitude, joy, and love flowed through me.

Gratitude is the unseen force that leads to manifestation. Gratitude opened the way for my vision to unfold.

Part
I

The Circle

*"Never doubt that a small group of thoughtful,
committed citizens can change the world.
Indeed, it is the only thing that ever has."*
—Generally attributed to Margaret Mead

Since that first call, A Community of Transformation (ACT) has been operating from a Circular Leadership model, based on principles described in this book. Although we have seen many changes over the years, the model has stayed fairly consistent and the organization is considered successful.

This first section is about The Circle: the heart of the model. It contains insights on the experience, potential, and effects of participating in a circle, especially one that was envisioned as a way for a group of people to change the world.

Chapter 1

A Window into the Story of ACT: How do you Successfully Belong to a Group?

—*Vicki Fearey*

We sit in a circle. It's always a circle. There are twelve of us. Not a magic number, but it is our number. We always begin with a check in, a connection. It is always different but always similar. Sometimes it is a question. Sometimes each person gets a word. However we start the activity, it provides a few minutes for each person to share current happenings, challenges, sufferings, if you will: the good, the not so good. We hear each other's stories, feel their feelings, listen to their teachings, look into their world. We each take the others in and see more clearly parts of ourselves. Each month the rituals happen. The more we do it the better we get at doing it succinctly, quickly, meaningfully, deeply. We silently send the speaker appreciation, compassion and love. And then the meeting's business agenda begins.

It is a meeting of Circular Leadership with the intent to not only accomplish the business at hand but also to spiral each person upward. Perhaps spiraling upward is not so much an intent as a result of the process. Steven Covey, American author, international educator and professional speaker, would say the upward spiral is universally recognized as a symbol for growth. In our organization, ACT (A Community of Transformation), we think there is no better way to achieve our goals of arranging speakers and events for personal transformation.

We promote emotional balance. One nervous system calms another. As business issues get decided and resolved, we are *emotionally* engaged not just cognitively engaged. We are responsive to each other, both intellectually and emotionally. This connection is woven through the evening and the meeting ends with another ritual, which is like the ending of a musical movement. It brings the crescendo to a positive resolution that each person takes home.

The business of the meeting covers the nuts and bolts of the speaker event: publicity/marketing, registration, location logistics—the topics of many organizations. Our circle is a microcosm of the world. There are fast thinkers and fast talkers, slow processers, big picture people, detail people, the person who ponders long and deep, the person of many words, the person of few words. All are in the circle—different ages, different professions, different backgrounds—a diverse circle. But the genius of it is coming together in a circular way. Our combined abilities elevate and strengthen us. We come together with a healthy dose of humility—a knowing that we are all necessary and no one is better.

Some of the components that are present are creativity, trust, non-judgment, collaboration, shared vision, shared values, a consensus decision-making style, commitment, empathy, interpersonal awareness and inclusion. The key to ensuring that such qualities are present in the circle is the concept of openness to hear each other, accept, and expand or refine whatever and however the person shows up. Every person in the circle has a teaching with their way of being, their ideas and their way of understanding. It is as if each person is a mirror reflecting back to each other parts of ourselves. The Circular Leadership model, in which every voice is heard and no one is discriminated against, is a leadership style which takes us to the growing edge of our own self-awareness. The whole is always greater than the sum of its parts.

Circular Leadership, when accomplished with humility, respect, non-judgment and empathy, becomes intrapersonal and interpersonal. The members relate to each other while taking in and realizing that part of himself or herself is being reflected back. The process of Circular Leadership is experiential learning. There is an aspect to it that becomes known only through the doing. Perhaps like parenting. Or journeying with a dying person. The word *Gnostic* seems to apply. It comes from the Greek word *gnotikos*, meaning *of knowledge* or *to know*, like the Gnostic gospels. People who have the knowledge are those who have lived it.

What makes a support group effective and supportive? What makes it spiral upwards? What makes it transformative? We each come into the circle as individuals with needs, feelings, and the grand physiology of the human body—a physiology with which we bring a vulnerability that gives us a need to know that we are accepted and understandable. We often find such support in our personal relationships, but there are many times when a tribe (family) is not enough. So, we seek groups that fill the gaps in the upwardly spiraling lift of our souls. When we gather in the circle of the ACT Council there is a distinct sense of connection. The opening ritual generates the feelings of the safe haven. As we share, there is a sense that wherever you are is okay. Our joys are shared and our distresses seem more manageable. After we connect, we start on the business at hand with a greater sense of accepted competence.

As in many healthy support groups, the rhythm of Circular Leadership is a sense of self that flows between dissonances to a secure sense of self. One might think, "Oh, I have talked too much." Or, "I don't have anything worthwhile to contribute." Or,

"I have missed the mark." But in a circular, upwardly spiraling group, the intentional sense of connection promoted by acceptance and positive responsiveness makes the harmony flow back invisibly toward each member of the group. The invisible becomes visible in the subtle way each person sits, moves and, most importantly, contributes creatively. Feeling *good enough* to show up fully is what we do for each other. In a reversed way, it is like Winnicott's theory of the good enough mother. Donald Winnicott, a British pediatrician and psychoanalyst, coined the phrase, "good enough mother" in 1953[1]. His concept is based on the idea that a child can develop a healthy sense of self and healthy coping skills in the presence of a good enough mother or, in other words, an imperfect mother. The *good enough* concept can be applied here. We are able to tolerate and accept our imperfections because the group accepts and values our state of *good enoughness*. It's okay to be vulnerable. It's okay not to be perfect. It's good for the group to be *good enough*. This takes the group to a higher level of cohesiveness, effectiveness, and creativity, and, therefore, to a higher level of spirituality, if you will.

Some groups in our culture bond through a common problem, which is often deeply beneficial and healing. Examples are grief groups, groups centered around health challenges, or community problems. Circular Leadership is like a spiritual business model. In the process of event planning for transformational purposes the CCC (Co-Creation Council) *grows* each other. We are uplifted, connected, and a little stronger. What would our world look like if all our groups had this model? We live in a world of thoughts, feelings and emotions. A person or organization can make decisions based on facts and logic and still understand that a lay off or a firing, for example, does not feel good. Consider the cartoon depicting a not uncommon situation in corporate America. The grim reaper, tall with his black hooded cape and scythe, walks through a sea of workstations until he arrives at his destination cubicle. Looking over the partition and down on the shrinking employee he says, "If I can make this anymore humiliating just let me know." Then the poor man or woman is escorted to the door with a little box of personal possessions.

Or consider the common linear leadership style of many organizations in this culture that attempts to address low morale. One particular situation comes to mind. I was working for a large corporation and morale was very low. People had been let go in a controversial manner, staffing was lean, and the work load was high. An upper level corporate manager came from another state for the purpose of de-escalating malcontent and letting the staff have an opportunity to talk about the problems. However, the main phrase of the manager's communication was, "You shouldn't feel that way." Needless to say, the wisdom of the group could not be tapped. Nor was it a management style that helped us grow.

Through my years of employment, I've experienced many staff meetings where the feeling was very different from the acceptance of Circular Leadership. Ideas were turned down or worse, ignored. Problems were primary topics with corrective action plans as the main focus rather than a synergy of upward growth.

Consider the linear manager style based on exclusion of information. A popular management theory advocates the dissemination of information on a need-to-know-basis. Often the result is the formation of subgroups, *in* groups and *out* groups, or the popular and the not popular, like cliques in high school. In Circular Leadership the feel is different. A germane point of Circular Leadership is the feel of the process, and its main consideration is its ability to *grow* the people in the circle. Many companies and organizations are shifting to this wisdom but the human ego's desire for power in America's corporate culture still remains dominant.

All of us are in groups and, on a conscious or unconscious level, we lead or follow or do a combination of the two. We may live in a family, we may live alone, but usually there are people in our sphere: family members, extended family members, work groups, committees, friends, neighbors. A group who works closely together, whether as a work group, a family group, or a committee, has a style. Take a close look. What is the style? Is it circular or linear? But the most important question is does it make you grow? How so? Does it influence you to contribute, to give and to receive respect, to listen, and to have empathy? And how does it make you feel? Does the group embody the feeling that if one succeeds, we all succeed? How does it make the members grow? And now go to the next step. How do you take that experience into the world? Do you contribute to others because of the experience?

In prior centuries there have been civilizations, groups that seem to have more elements of Circular Leadership than the often ego-driven large corporations of today. Tribal circles with rituals of spirituality and inclusion may be an example. The twelve disciples of Jesus could reflect a management style of growth and inclusion. Perhaps the growth of Circular Leadership organizations, where relationships come first, is like someone walking up a set of stairs while working a yoyo. The yoyo goes up and down but eventually, because growth-oriented groups affect other groups, we all end up on a higher step.

Vicki Fearey

Vicki Fearey is a licensed clinical professional counselor with a focus on healing from grief and loss. She works as a bereavement coordinator for Heartland Hospice and as a psychotherapist in private practice. She blends her training as a certified life coach and a certified hypnotherapist into her practice. She is an advanced

Reiki practitioner and a registered yoga teacher. Her focus is on helping people to grow holistically and spiritually. Vicki has served on the ACT Council in the Annapolis area for three years.

Notes:

1. Donald Winnicott, Playing and Reality, Tavistock Publications, ISBN: 9780415345464

Chapter 2

Line Management Evolves to Circle Management

—Richard Bredeson

"Line in nature is not found;
Unit and universe are round;
In vain produced, all rays return;
Evil will bless, and ice will burn."

Quoting Uriel from a poem, *Uriel* by Ralph Waldo Emerson.

The central thesis of Archangel Uriel, according to Emerson in his poem written in 1846, is the absence of the line in the Universe. This is a disruptive notion that upsets the pantheon of "young deities," Angels, "old war-gods" and demi-gods; their reaction sends Uriel, at least temporarily, into a funk.

This idea of line *versus* round is evolutionary. I believe Emerson was ahead of his time; he caused quite a stir among his religious superiors and peers in his day.

This evolution that Emerson promotes is clearly seen in the evolution of management styles and philosophies of our modern era. And my central thesis is to promote the superiority of management within the "round" over management by "line."

Throughout my career in management within multiple organizations for several companies and government, on divergent projects and programs, I have seen, experienced and used several approaches to accomplish objectives through managing teams of people. Much of this experience is with "line" organizations. Let's begin by defining and exploring that experience.

Line Management refers to the management of a product or service line. I suspect the term originates from the manufacturing world and the management of an assembly line or process. From the Industrial Revolution onward lines have been created to accomplish objectives by people whether they are assembling components for a piece of hardware, creating components for a software program, synthesizing substances for a pharmaceutical company, or amalgamating data streams for an information product. And line managers are the people directly responsible for the production line. Wikipedia defines *line manager* this way:

"A line manager is an employee who directly manages other employees and operations while reporting to a higher-ranking manager." Notice the hierarchy built into this definition. A hierarchy in turn is a line that can be drawn directly from the bottommost employee all the way through the layers of management to the top person in charge of the entire operation.

I began my career in the corporate world after several years teaching, as a computer software programmer. I was assigned a component of software to build. I reported to an analyst responsible for the entire program. And he reported to a manager responsible for a complete set of programs operating a database. And he reported to a director who was responsible for the database and operations using that database. And ... well, you get the picture. From that one software component a larger and larger *product* was built to support the overall operations of the enterprise.

Over a ten-year span I rose through this hierarchy, until I was managing all of the programs and those who built and maintained the software assembled into those programs for the entire data operations of the enterprise. And this organization succeeded in accomplishing the established objectives. Lines of communications were clear and direct.

Through this time and several more positions with other companies with different objectives, usually involving computer programming in one form or another, always involving managing other people, I examined and experimented with different management *styles*. Still, these styles, for the most part, fit within a hierarchy: a *line* organization. Examples of these styles, as first documented by Douglas McGregor[1], are "Theory X" and "Theory Y" approaches.

Essentially Theory X fits very well in the hierarchical line management approach. It assumes workers are not particularly self-motivated on the job and therefore need close supervision. It is clearly a top-down approach to achieving objectives through a group of people. It is a measured and measuring approach.

Theory Y, on the other hand, assumes workers are motivated to do a good job and can even contribute their own ideas and creativity when encouraged to do so. This is more of a bottom up approach, where teams of workers are given objectives and resources, then left to their own creativity and ingenuity to accomplish the desired results.

Then in the 80s the Japanese Management Approach, sometimes dubbed "Theory Z," became popular, especially because the quality factor for products was markedly improved. For example, the quality of Japanese cars was clearly superior to those manufactured in the US by *old-style* line management approaches. Theory Z takes Theory Y a step farther and creates a worker-centric organization in which the workers' well-being, creativity and input into the production process are emphasized. With this approach the employees have ownership in not only the quality of the finished product but in all aspects of the creative process, from conception through realization.

You can see the evolution in these theories from work-centric to worker-centric philosophies. And each approach has its place within organizations. In my experience, if a product deadline is tight, budget limited, resources restricted then Theory X can be effective. I used a Theory Y approach in managing a software project in the late 70s. The team had some great ideas and kicked around different strategies to create the most efficient approach while minimizing computer resources (this was in the days of giant rooms-full of computing equipment). The trouble started when the schedule and budget began to pinch. The shift to Theory X to get the job done became imperative.

There are good examples where Theory Z has been effective. The anecdotal evidence from companies like Microsoft and Google, where employees are central to the organizations, have great work environments, have access to child-care, and many other benefits to foster loyalty and commitment to the company, indicates the superiority of this management style to foster creativity and innovation.

Is Theory Z the end of the *line* when it comes to management approaches? Perhaps it is, because in my continuing experience it is the *circle* that is an evolutionary step beyond *line management*. I turn now to the description and benefits of Circle Management –

the superiority over *line* proposed by Emerson through the voice of Uriel.

I have been active within a Management Circle for the past several years. I am the webmaster for A Community of Transformation (ACT) and sit on the ACT board, called the Co-Creation Council (CCC), not as a voting member but as an observer, noting any actions to be taken as lead technologist for the organization's communications, both internally and externally. The CCC meets in circle when conducting the business of the organization.

In the Circle every member of the Council has equal standing. There are officers of the organization self-selected each year and serving for at least a one-year term. One of these officers is self-selected as the Chair of the CCC, responsible to take the lead, set agendas, establish programs and conduct the general business of ACT; but all actions and directions are taken in Circle with full consensus of all members. This organizational style and management approach has proven to be very effective in successfully guiding the growth and evolution of ACT for nearly two decades.

In Circle, each member has a voice, a responsibility, an authority and the respect of each of the other members. There is a complete and equal democratic sense to this organization. And it is even fun to watch it in action as the work of ACT gets done. I will leave it to others to describe in more detail how this Circle operates, how the dynamics flow, what the critical components of the Circle's functions are and implementation details that keep it balanced and moving. I am more interested in exploring why this organization works, why it is superior to *line* management.

To begin by quoting Uriel again: "Unit and universe are round." I find it fascinating that Emerson wrote this 170 years ago and modern science is describing all of creation (the unit and the universe) as a *hologram*. If the building block of the universe is a *holon*, doesn't it make sense that a hologram makes an excellent model for an organizational structure? A *holon*, a term coined by Arthur Koestler[2] in 1967, to describe something that is both a whole thing and at the same time a part of something else (a whole/part), is then how the universe is constructed. As Ken Wilber[3] points out in his *A Brief History of Everything*, "reality is composed neither of things nor processes, neither wholes nor parts, but whole/parts, or holons—all the way up and all the way down." And, importantly, Jude Currivan[4] in her *The Cosmic Hologram, Information at the Center of Creation,* points out that, "human beings in both space and time act holographically."

My experience of the ACT Co-Creation Council gathering and operating in circle does act holographically. And if the cosmos is a hologram, we are holograms; then the Council Circle is also a hologram. This, then, is the natural way to operate. There is the power of the cosmos in the operation of the ACT governing body!

Let's dig into this a little deeper. As individuals, holons within the Circle, we each bring our individual skills, talents, understandings, motivations, objectives, beliefs, prejudices, foibles, basically our personalities, into the Circle. Then in joining the Circle a new Holon is formed; we each, as our own whole/part, become a member of the Circle the next level up on the *holon scale* – also called *holarchy.* The Circle is a new thing, a new whole/part. It is whole as in the governing body of ACT and it is a part as in a subset of the membership and community of ACT, yet another Holon. The important feature here is that the CCC as a Holon is far more powerful than any of the individuals forming the Circle.

The Circle is more creative, more energetic, more motivated, more innovative, more of just about any characteristic of any one individual. And I have found that many of the negative characteristics we as individuals may bring to the Circle get softened, modified, even eliminated in Circle. In short, our strengths are amplified and others compensate our weaknesses in Circle. This is a synergistic effect that creates strong leadership for a dynamic, growing and evolving organization.

In her book, *Calling the Circle,* essentially an instruction manual for implementing Circle Management, Christina Baldwin[5] describes three cultures that she has observed through her work. She describes First Culture as indigenous or native culture in operation from the beginning of time. Her experience and observations in her delightful book are that First Cultures operate in Circle. Their society, their government, their organizational leadership tend toward a "circle-style" of management. I have experienced this indirectly through my reading and through teachers of indigenous cultures, particularly the Mayan culture of Guatemala as carried by Martín Prechtel[6]. In his books, especially *Secrets of the Talking Jaguar: Memoirs from the Living Heart of a Mayan Village*, Martín describes his life among the Mayans of Santiago Atitlan where he studied with the chief Shaman of the village and became a community elder. The community was governed by a Council of Elders who met in Circle.

Second Culture, as defined by Baldwin, is what I have described above as line management. It is hierarchical, structured very much along the lines we live with today. We live for the most part as members of Second Culture. It is what Uriel decries as "in nature is not found." First Culture is "natural" while Second Culture is not.

Baldwin's Third Culture is managed within Circle. And I can almost see this as a return, a *circling back* to First Culture! Why? There is something natural about the Circle. Emerson had it right. One could almost see this as *Divine Order*. Is this the power of the Circle; is this the source of the effectiveness of Circle Management?

I am reminded of a cartoon strip created by Bill Keane in the 60s and now continued by his son, *The Family Circus*. Remember that format, the big circle in which the characters were drawn? I always thought of the family as a circle. Maybe it's the first circle of our experience. My experience now as a member of the ACT Council meeting in Circle is that of *family*. And, yes, sometimes it does feel like a *circus*. But it is powerful, effective, creative and dynamic in its call to enrich the lives of our community through transformation.

Proof of the effectiveness of the circle within which we manage ACT gets personal for me. Not long ago we were honoring Linda Roebuck, she who called the Circle in 2001, by going around saying a few words about her special gifts and work on behalf of ACT. When it was my turn I simply said, "You and ACT saved my life." I went on to tell the story of one of my first ACT meetings. Our speaker that afternoon was an acupuncturist and Qigong teacher. To conclude her talk she led us through a simple Qigong form for health, longevity and peace. From that moment I was hooked. I went on to take classes from her, then from her teacher, and then I became qualified to teach others.

To this day I study, practice and teach Qigong, an ancient Chinese approach to health. In 2017, I had a heart attack; it actually occurred while I was doing Qigong! It was not dramatic, no dropping to my knees. My wife drove me to the hospital and I walked in for tests. To keep the story short, within a few days I had open-heart surgery to improve blood flow to my heart. My recovery was rapid; doctors and nurses were amazed. I owe my life, my continued well-being, my path, to Qigong, which I discovered through ACT. My life was, and continues to be, transformed.

I began with a poem; I'll end with one to praise once more the power of a circle and five important virtues that hold it, mold it and keep it sacred:

Human Virtues
by Richard Bredeson

Love:
It all begins with love,
The creating force alive
Through the whole world
From deepest deep to highest above.

Honor:
A state of being derived from love,
Self-love, the source of all;
A principle that upholds, ennobles,
Creating the foundation for Human.

Integrity:
Springing from honor, Human
Knows place in the world; holds
Space firmly on that foundation;
Rises to each occasion to bless.

Community:
Integral Human reaches outward
To serve humanity in blessed community.
Community blesses Human in sacred symmetry
Echoing voices of goddesses and gods.

High Purpose:
The highest purpose is to love,
Honor, grow in integrity, serve
Community in a spiral blessing rising
Through the evolution of Humanity.

Richard Bredeson

Richard Bredeson is both a technologist and a healer. He maintains several websites for both ACT and his and his wife's businesses and church. As a healer he studies, practices and teaches Qigong, an ancient Chinese approach to health, happiness and longevity. He is a non-voting member of the ACT Co-Creation Council that meets in Circle. Richard is also a poet working on several collections to be published soon and published on his blog: MenandtheGoddess.com.

Notes:

1. Douglas McGregor, The Human Side of Enterprise, McGraw-Hill Education, ISBN: 9780071462228

2. Arthur Koestler, The Ghost in the Machine, Last Century Media, ISBN: 9781939438348

3. Ken Wilber, A Brief History of Everything, Shambala, ISBN:157062187X

4. Jude Currivan, The Cosmic Hologram, Information at the Center of Creation, Inner Traditions ISBN: 9781620556603

5. Christina Baldwin, Calling the Circle, Bantam Press, ISBN: 9780553379006

6. Martín Prechtel, Secrets of the Talking Jaguar: Memoirs from the Living Heart of a Mayan Village, Jeremy P. Tarcher/ Penquin, ISBN: 9780874779707

Chapter 3

Expansive Inclusivity
—J. Arthur

Many moons ago, the wisdom of the elders was valued, sunrises were appreciated, and the phases of life were embraced and fully lived. The earth-honoring agrarian societies of old lived in balance with seasonal cycles, and those individuals were in harmony with their own nature. This innate awareness has been negated in deference to our productivity, which is acknowledged in the common truism that no one lays on their deathbed wishing they had spent more time at the office.

Circular Leadership is not new, yet recognizing it, understanding its strengths, and thriving within it may be new to us. The concept itself fosters a blend of empowerment and cooperation, and is therefore both expansive and inclusive. This is most easily recognizable as the tribal approach, wherein countless prehistoric generations flourished before individuals isolated themselves atop pyramids of policies and procedures. Mankind has seen progress and advances in technology and science, yet we still intrinsically yearn for connection and a meaningful sense of balance.

Today we see where Circular Leadership is re-emerging. Teamwork is supplanting time management. Management criterion is slowly shifting away from making people better employees toward making employees better people. The pendulum is swinging. This very notion of shared authority challenges the hierarchical structure wherein power is isolated at the top.

These systems succeeded by holding authority at the apex while being supported by rigid compliance. Eventually, however, the emperor has no clothes... This style of linear leadership is ultimately ineffective beyond the immediate objective. Coveting power over others must eventually, and is, indeed, giving way to sharing empowerment with like-minded, open-hearted companions, and this is accomplished through conscious communication.

The English language is wonderful! Complex without being too complicated, and having a vocabulary of over two million words, it's amazing how playful we can be with it. Past civilizations are respected for their development of written language, just as one day a future anthropologist might ponder our ability to …

drive on a parkway and park on a driveway, or ... have noses that run and feet that smell. Language empowers us to define our reality, whether a toddler says, "No!" to its mother, or an oppressed people say, "No More!" to a dictator. Empowerment through sharing ideas, creativity, interconnectedness, compassion and more are all achieved by how we use language.

We can find modern day cases where this pyramid of power has been inverted and the resultant system is actually thriving. The twelve-step approach to recovery, as a prime example, is based on a deliberate absence of authority beyond *God's will*. Here, all decisions are made through a collective *group consciousness* sharing process. The United Nations, likewise, functions with a revolving chairmanship, which serves cooperatively. This global collective monitors and verifies civility, then polices through sanctions, thus proving many times over how the *pen is truly mightier than the sword*. Our own American petri dish of democracy is based on language, wherein the principles expressed are valued more so than the personalities who've expressed them. Similarly, academia and medical science advance methodically through peer-review of published conclusions. Each of these organizations and associations are, in fact, leaderless, yet has established its viability on the premise of respectful cooperation, service to a higher purpose, and accountability to future generations. Moreover, these societal institutions change slowly, which proves to be a hallmark of their resilience. Their effectiveness broadens across time, sustained by the very diversity that would threaten typical linear leadership.

Dynamic individuals do occasionally step up to the lectern and give the pendulum a heartfelt push. We witnessed this in Spring 2018 when several dozen high school students stood up and spoke up following a tragic and senseless shooting at their school in Florida. "NO MORE!" they admonished, as they marched in protest and solidarity, willing to become spark plugs in an Engine of Transformation for School Safety. In a moment of feeling powerless, they found their common voice and inspired tens of thousands around the world to "March for Our Lives" and "Stand with The Students."

These moments when hearts come together for a cause are only possible because there is not any one person in charge, no organized structure of leadership. Individuals act from their heart and their convictions to initiate change which matters to them. We decide at various points in our lives to become willing participants rather than passive observers.

This is what makes ACT Annapolis such a dynamic aspect of the growth of consciousness expansion within our area. It serves as an incubator for metaphysicians and new-thought facilitators. It promotes connection, yet embraces diversity and change, hence the name: A Community of Transformation.

A is not *The*. *A* invites us to consider possibilities and accommodate differences. Here, an option is implied, or perhaps several, wherein there are opportunities to have a preference. *A* allows for discernment, choice, and space where any one particular path is not *the* only way. *Community* can best be understood in this context as a contraction for *common unity*. We repurpose this word here and broaden its meaning beyond *our community*, beyond geographic neighborhoods and other familiar ethnic, usually divisive connotations. Rather, we embrace a shared intent within a *common unity* of purpose, which might be simply stated as living deliberately, peacefully and lovingly. We show up, conscious and aware, willing to creatively express our gifts and hold sacred the space of empowerment. We find inspiration through our alignment with these higher visions. We openly encourage others to live more fully, which serves to further enliven this expansive energy throughout our own lives.

Transformation is the process by which something is changed, and the thing in this instance is our *selves*. We move our thoughts, beliefs, and choices from wherever they are toward a *form* which is intrinsically more useful. Now, no one can quite say what inspires a caterpillar to embrace itself in a cocoon. Through this process each caterpillar transcends its past, forms a new reality, and continues its life at what we would perceive to be a higher vibration. One butterfly, however, does not change all of the other caterpillars; each one must undergo its own process. We don't isolate ourselves in a chrysalis, but rather this emerging reality first forms in our mind and our consciousness, passes through our heart, and only then might we allow it to manifest. As we transform our *selves* and begin to live as expressions of our true, higher nature it's not unlike a butterfly spreading its beautiful new wings. We awaken from within our energetic chrysalis to radiate these higher states of being, like ripples in a pond, and this in turn raises the potentials for everyone around us.

ACT Annapolis is a safe haven for *spiritual butterflies* who are willing to have a positive impact. Each of us has experienced powerful transformative influences that have drawn more from us than we might have thought possible. Each of us has been, and are even now, as we co-author this book, is being transformed, and we value this common unity through which we are allowing our lives to be of service to a higher purpose. We welcome with gratitude the opportunity for Spirit to express itself through us, and together we celebrate the life, light, and Love flowing throughout our lives. (I believe the word Love deserves to always be capitalized…)

A mouse's ability to solve the maze dramatically increases once you drop in the cat, and so it may be with us; perhaps we inherently accomplish more whenever we're duly challenged or inspired. We tend to become too comfortable while we're tucked safely into our quiet, complacent lives. We often try to get all the pieces on our chess board lined up just right, yet this very notion seems to invite the winds of Spirit to begin to blow. We are called from within to become involved, to put down the remote and get up off the couch.

I have always (…well, mostly) lived for the adventure. Dancing into the unknown, going rogue, and diving in head first usually turn out to be the most fun expressions of willingness. Through participating in A Course in Miracles[1] study groups I've heard it said, "…if you want unconditional Love you must first place no conditions on who or what you Love," and I Love Life! When I was asked as a child, "What do you want to be when you grow up?" my answer was always, "Happy!" Now, I cannot stay in this idealistic consciousness all the time, of course, yet I do say, "Yes!" as often as possible. I answer the phone with, "Yes, hello…?" I start my emails with, "Yes, …" and my wife has even suggested I change my voicemail greeting from "Yes, this is Jim…" so I might be home a bit more. So, there's clearly a need to maintain balance, yet I believe, as author and motivational speaker Les Brown[2] suggests in his audio publication; "You can die on the field or you can die in the bleachers, so why not come down onto the field and have a good time?"

When Linda approached me and invited me to become involved in ACT Annapolis, my life was already careening through transformation. I had recently moved from rural Texas where, if someone honked their horn at you at one of the dozen or so red lights in town, it was because they hadn't seen you in a while and they were smiling and waving. I quickly learned how Annapolis and DC area drivers don't usually operate from this mindset. I wasn't discouraged, though. I knew why I had moved, it was to be near my mother during her twilight years. I am so grateful I said, "Yes," to this life-changing opportunity, yet what I didn't know then was the profound wisdom of God's timing. My sister's cancer diagnosis came just eight months after I moved from Texas, and it was such an incredible blessing to be present and available for my mother as she lost her youngest daughter.

My brother-in-law's and mother's deaths came within the next year, and I crumbled from within as I gathered the shattered pieces of my world. I embraced the grieving process as best I could, shoved everything into storage, moved into a basement studio efficiency, and focused on self-care and keeping my job. Even then, I referred to what I was going through as my *cocoon time*, and my new friends within ACT (and my new church-home, Unity by The Bay) allowed me my healing time yet encouraged me to get back onto my feet. While I still tear up when I recall the sound of my mother sobbing "... Nooo," as they closed her daughter's casket lid, I've grown to appreciate even more the precious gift of time that was available only because I took the spiritual leap of faith, said, "Yes," and moved from Texas.

Time, it seems, does indeed heal, and I've since stabilized, married my new best friend, and reconnected with my adult son, his awesome wife, and my two beautiful grandchildren. Each day these new butterfly wings become stronger and more colorful as my evolving transformation continues with creative writing, continuing my higher education, and an entry-level management position at my work. I've also allowed a transformation to occur in my perception of God. I've shifted my paradigm away from one where I am trying to have more faith. Now, I set my intention to be the kind of man in whom God might have faith. Further, I attend church now in order to get my answers questioned, rather than the other way around. I'm also growing to appreciate how the Native Americans refer to God as "The Great Mystery", thus acknowledging the omnipresence of a Loving Great Spirit without presuming to understand it.

My involvement within ACT Annapolis was instrumental in my getting back up on my feet throughout my grieving and recovery, which has been my *real* transformation beyond just moving from Texas. The Love, safety, and sense of connection that sustained me through those devastating months has been transcendent.

I'd learned through experience how Love gets in through the cracks in our heart whenever it breaks. This is exactly what occurred with my becoming engaged and inviting my new *family of choice* to dance at my wedding. Jenevieve had a front-row seat during my grieving process, saw through my pain and drama, waited patiently, and invited me to shed my chrysalis and step into a loving, expansive, conscious relationship. With us both being empty-nesters, and each having been single quite a while, we believed we were ready to form a new bond of connection and commitment. We created our dream-come-true wedding, wrote our own vows, and christened our church's new sanctuary with music, feasting, laughter, and joy.

We committed, not only to each other, but to a higher sense of purpose, which we prayed our relationship might serve. We sought to create a sacred space together, where others would feel safe and inspired whenever they were near us. We spoke daily in those early months of how we would never be *here* again, exploring and facing those precious moments of newness when romance is delicate. We knew how our stepping forward together and saying, "Yes!" as a couple meant that it would not just be *us* entering into this relationship. We were merging our circles of friends with our newly blended families, and we were in turn asking for their heartfelt commitment to uphold and support us and our marriage.

We co-created a visualization, imagining ourselves sitting on a heavenly park bench preparing to commit as a holy Archangel of Relationship fluttered its wings and settled down between us. Then, enfolding us within the safety of its wingspan said, "Yes, welcome. I am here with you, beside you, to dance with you and to guide you. You seek to embark on this sacred relationship, and with this choice you invite me to join you. For this union, to be sanctified, shall serve a higher purpose than you can know. You invite Love into your midst, yet truly, you are entering a flowing river that will move you beyond yourselves. Love will both empower you and purify you. Love seeks to uplift and inspire, and your new marriage will be its own, for you will be Love's stewards on this sacred journey." Ever since, each of us has grown in ways we couldn't have anticipated. We marvel at how we continue to enhance each other's lives, and how blessed we are when we keep our focus on serving Spirit.

The nature of leadership within ACT Annapolis is encompassing and open-hearted self-guidance, perhaps similar to what the Native Americans shared when they sat in council around their moonlit campfires. ACT's governance is styled much more like the spokes of a wheel, rather than the rungs of a ladder. Each person's opinions and feelings are valued, each voice is heard, time is allowed for contemplation, and shared consensus is prioritized. Toes cannot get stepped on when everyone is swimming in the warm waters of mutual respect, appreciation, and integrity. Decisions are inclusive and core values are embraced.

It is my pleasure and joy to contribute to this continuation of ACT's expansive vision. We've discussed within our monthly ACT Council meetings how what we've done can be duplicated. ACT Annapolis could serve as a (...*a*, not *the*) model for other visionaries who are seeking another way. Today there are a comfortable number of members and friends who are participants in ACT Annapolis. We've matured within our geographic cocoon, and publishing this book represents the spreading of our butterfly wings.

One of my favorite quotes, often attributed to clergyman Robert Schuller, is, "You can count the seeds in an apple, yet you can't count the apples in a seed." This book is the seed which we are casting forth into the fertile soil of your heart and mind. We've known the time is right, and we're willing to expand our reality to include you. Yes, you! Why re-invent the wheel? I believe if you've read this far then you already know...

We each have the opportunity, or better stated, the *spiritual appointment*, to BE the change we want to see in the world. I would venture to guess there are at least five people whom you've thought about while you were reading this book who have the potential to be spokes in your own ACT wheel. Each of these friends has their unique blend of gifts and their unique perspectives, yet likely also shares many common core values with you. It's not a question of whether they would be willing to show up with you in the co-creation of an ACT in your city. The key question now is whether you will consider saying, "Yes," to this opportunity. I invite you to dare to be willing, to dare to say, "Yes!" to stretch your boundaries and dare to ask others to join in a Council Consciousness and explore what might be possible. Who knows, the next time someone honks at you at a red light, they just might be smiling and waving because they're glad to see you.

J. Arthur

Little Jimmy went swimming every day, and when it was too cold he'd either be canoeing or fishing. Frogs, tadpoles, crawdads, and other creek-critters knew to hide especially well once his grade school let out each day. Watercolor sunsets preceded the bats, lightning bugs, and sometimes, the owls. Later, stargazing, meteors, and the occasional satellite were always best after moonset. For him, there was always a day full of time for everything he did.

Notes:

1. A Course in Miracles, A Foundation for Inner Peace: https://acim.org,
2. You Deserve: Les Brown, ISBN: 9606388-9-X

Part
II

The Model in Practice

"Coming together is a beginning; keeping together is progress; working together is success"
— Attributed to both Henry Ford and Edward Everett Hale

There is no formula or predefined process for how to implement a Circular Leadership model in an organization. It is more like a recipe that has been passed down from generation to generation. Each new recipient makes changes based on their tastes or what ingredients are available. If there is an understanding of the role of each ingredient (e.g., leavening agent) and the intent of any direction (e.g., stir just until combined), then substitutions or changes can be made and still produce the desired output (e.g., a cake).

As people or intentions change, the model may organically evolve as well. That is why it is appropriate to think of this model as a framework – or recipe – for implementing Circular Leadership principles in a manner that is best suited to your group. The different spiritual practices, beliefs, interests, and perspectives of the members of your group will ultimately define how you will communicate, connect, and collaborate.

This section highlights the recipe that has been implemented by the Co-Creation Council of ACT. It provides insights into the processes and roles, as well as showcases how steps in that process match different philosophical and spiritual beliefs held by our members. It is this interplay between individual beliefs and group practices that keeps the circular model relevant. The implementation may change in response to the members, but the intent behind the activities stays the same.

Chapter 4

Leading from Within:
Role of the Leader in Circle
—Linda Roebuck

What is the role of a leader in a circle of leaders? The overwhelming response to my having called The First Circle left me filled with gratitude. I was then filled with questions: How was I supposed to lead the amazing group of leaders who had shown up? What characteristics would I need to cultivate and demonstrate? When would I step in? When would I step back?

A basic requirement for success is to know who's in charge of your life. Are you the one running the show, or do you believe that a higher power has the ultimate control over your life? Gaining clarity and peace on this question reveals your potential for being a successful leader.

Knowing my purpose required delving into key questions: Who am I? Why am I here? I still ask those questions as I continue to evolve. I believe the role of an effective leader calls for continuous inner work, questioning beliefs, and releasing limiting thoughts and patterns. It's about getting real with myself and looking at all my strengths, qualities and character traits, both negative and positive.

What I quickly learned about leading a circle of leaders was how I must first be the leader of my own circle, of my own self. This meant letting go of my expectations and acknowledging that I wasn't in charge. My not being in charge meant surrendering to what was in charge: the Divine within. My role was to maintain my own connection to Source; to hold space for others to connect; and, to set the intention and boundaries so everyone in the circle could comfortably show up and fully play their part. My role was not to lead the group, but to occasionally guide the energy that empowers the group.

There wasn't enough structure and definition in those early months for the group to take ownership of its path. Someone needed to lead them through the process for the initial steps. Since this was my vision they had shown up for, it was to be my responsibility in those early meetings to define, unify, and evolve the conversations into a shared vision.

My inner challenge was to quiet my human self, or personality, who wants to be in control, to seek approval, recognition, and acceptance by others. To separate my needs from the needs of the circle, I learned about a different type of discernment, primarily how to discern what is *not* mine to do. Often, I had to discern how to support the members of the group so that they could self-identify their own contributions or roles on any particular topic. Things flowed naturally, once I stopped trying to always define what was mine to do. My centering practice became a simple process with huge benefits: I would pause, take a breath, and go within. In the quiet moment I tuned inward, to what I call my *internal feeling barometer*, or my IFB. It always let me know if I was coming from a loving place or a fear-based place.

If I was trying to make something happen, worrying about how to get what I thought was right, or struggling to figure out why I had to play a role that wasn't aligned with truth, my IFB registered *fear*! Another issue that caused my IFB to be fearful was when I would think someone or something outside of me had to change. This was another opportunity for me to let go and to trust that our intention was being met or would be manifested.

When I found myself acting from a place of fear, I usually found an underlying feeling of not being good enough, smart enough, or worthy. I then made a conscious choice to shift to a more loving place – a place of self-love. Only then could I set the space for the circle from this place of love instead of bringing my fears into the mix. This forced me to develop a level of trust in myself that I had not previously known, one where I trusted that I was truly leading from within.

I was becoming our leader without taking away anyone else's power. For me this trust was anchored in a personal peace that comes from trusting in the Divine. By trusting the part of me that was one with the Divine it was easy to allow the perfect outcome to manifest. All I had to do was get out of my own way.

I've drawn strength from my past training and recalled how one of the first things I had to do in my coaching certification program was to develop a *purpose statement* based on peak experiences in my life. Key words were extracted from my descriptions and used to come up with my purpose. I memorized and repeated it often. It proclaims,

> "My purpose is to spread the Light by gathering Circles of Light using divine, feminine energy and intuitive knowing, in order to birth Higher Consciousness on the planet."

That was almost twenty years ago. Recently, I had shivers when I came across the paper where I had written it and realized, *Oh, Yes, I am on purpose!*

My role has been to lead by example; to trust and surrender; and to establish and hold space from a place of love. Then others can connect and act from a position of personal integrity and empowerment.

What is more profound is that in return for leading the circle, for being on this spiraling Circular Leadership journey with the group, I, too, have learned and grown with those who sit in my circle. That's the magic! Most often, the result was more magnificent than I could ever have thought possible.

I leave you with a personal declaration, which bubbled up as I remember my learning experience of leading a circle.

I stand powerfully with my circle in true humility, gratefully in service to the Power of Love, as together we wake up and rise!

Linda Roebuck

Linda founded A Community of Transformation (ACT), a non-profit educational organization, in 2001, whose focus is on holistic health: www.ActAnnapolis.org.

A teaching Usui and Karuna Reiki® Master, Linda is a gifted spiritual mentor, catalyst for change, and facilitator of remembering ancient knowledge. Her business, Linda Roebuck and Associates, LLC, offers programs, training, and individual sessions using the Alchemical Attunement and Activation (AAA) Healing© system she developed. Her website is www.LindaRoebuck.com.

Chapter 5

Creating the Culture of Circular Leadership
—*Carol Ann Robbins, PhD*

The culture of an organization is vital to its mission and purpose. The shared set of attitudes, values, goals and practices that characterize it are essential to its success. It is imperative to create a culture of evolution and transformation for each individual member as well as for the entire group. The essence of such a culture is to create a sacred circle of leadership within which all members are equally held in heart-centered regard in an energetic field of love. This creates a safe space to support authenticity, risk-taking, and creativity, to better benefit the group co-creation process for the leadership circle. How the members are (being) together is more important than what they do or accomplish, because successful belonging nurtures synergistic empowerment. Through collaboration and cooperation, we open our hearts to hear diverse ideas and perspectives, which strengthens us as a group and expands the realm of possibilities. We create a culture of heartfelt peace, love, respect and deep connection in a magical spiritual alchemy that holds us all in circle and allows us to love each other into wholeness. This love-based group consciousness and energy is experienced at a profound level rarely felt in typical linear leadership models.

So, how do we achieve all of this, one might ask? Let's start with describing an understanding of the shared attitudes, values and customs which underlie our group leadership gatherings. We are governed by a shared vision, purpose, mission and a set of universal operating principles, which together form our foundational culture. For our ACT (A Community of Transformation) organization, the essential vision is to be an inspirational, heart-centered community that nurtures profound transformation. We aim to create this at the global level, the community level, the leadership circle level, and at the individual level. Our mission is to assist individuals as they shift from focusing on a material and limited world to opening to a world of interconnected relationships and universal consciousness, co-creating the future of the world and the planet.

Basic Structure

We have established a twelve-member governing board, which we refer to as the Co-Creation Council (CCC). It can, perhaps, be likened to a circle of elders in indigenous communities. There is also a smaller Executive Team comprised of the primary leadership roles, or Officers, within the organization—Chair, Co-Chair, Treasurer, Scribe (secretary), and Program Chair—who meet separately, periodically, to attend to business which doesn't necessitate the entire board meeting. Committees are formed within the Board to manage various aspects of running the organization.

Prospective members contact the CCC when vacancies are announced, and they then engage in a process of discernment in self-selection to sit on the board. It is a very powerful process of self-inquiry that allows us each to tap into our intuitive knowing about the appropriateness of committing to serving in this capacity at this time in our lives. If we emerge from the discernment process with a clear mandate to join, we submit our application to join the CCC and the existing members approve the applicants using consensus. New members are then invited to an orientation process with the executive board and are given an ACT CCC Handbook. This orientation process engages the new members into the culture of the organization and the leadership circle.

Shared Values and Principles

Our operational values characterize the essence of the leadership circle, along with the universal principles at work through us. The key value for our group is that we believe in a power greater than ourselves that connects and unites the group. We refer to this group consciousness as the Soul of ACT. As described initially, we fundamentally believe in collaboration, cooperation, successful belonging and synergistic empowerment. We are stronger together as we open to diverse ideas and believe in member equality. All of us are teachers, learners, leaders, and healers whose individual divinity becomes amplified as a group. We believe in ongoing personal and interpersonal development, which is supported by board retreats and ACT workshops. We believe in the power of ritual—to gather us together in sacred space in support of group consciousness and to close our meetings in gratitude and appreciation.

The universal principles that inform our work are powered with Source energy and include the Power of Love, the Law of Intention, the Law of Attention, the Law of Attraction, the Law of Resonance, the Law of Manifestation, the Law of Divine Order, the Law of Coherence, the Law of Grace, and the Law of Energy, Frequency and Vibration, among others. These important key principles form the metaphysical basis of our work in Circular Leadership and transformation.

Practices and Customs

Our practices and customs are based on all of us embracing the Path of Integrity as individuals and as a group. This is the path to personal and collective fulfillment and successful accomplishment of our hopes and dreams.

Creating the sacred circle of engagement is the core practice of the Circular Leadership model. Setting the space is key to this process, which is done both physically in the arrangement of the meeting place and energetically. After a heartfelt exchange of hugs and greetings, Board meeting gatherings begin with an invitation to sit in circle and connect to the Soul of ACT with our shared intentions, tapping into the guidance coming in at that moment and honoring the feel of the energy in the room. An opening centering and connecting ritual then takes place, often involving listening to a spiritually meaningful song to raise the energy frequency and gather us in communion. We commonly follow up with a ritual that joins us all into connection through sharing (e.g., each drawing an oracle card and sharing how it resonates; each sharing a word describing how you feel right now and why; etc.). The energy in the room is honored and adjusted to, as needed, and we go into stillness to ground us each into full presence and heart-centered connection. This whole process creates a field of resonance and an amplification of energy as we energetically merge with one another into the oneness.

The business meeting is then initiated by looking at the agenda and beginning with the first item of business. As we move through the items at hand, we use several important practices to invite discernment, engaged listening, discussion, expansive inclusivity and consensus. When important decisions need to be made, our process is to invite engaged dialogue to share opinions and perspectives synergistically, as all options and possibilities are honored. We may then go into silence in an individual discernment process before voting on the outcome with a thumbs up, thumbs down, or thumbs sideways. We use consensus decision-making. This is a process by which everyone in a group is involved in a decision, and there is a group commitment towards success in implementing this decision. If there is not a unanimous consensus, we honor the differences and may further engage the members with concerns in sharing their thoughts, table the decision, and modify the group decision to incorporate the differences, if possible. Or members decide that they can live with a particular decision for the good of the group. Our foundational beliefs are that any obstacles that may arise are really miracles, or at least opportunities, in disguise that are there to teach us all. Consensus building, discernment and some of the rituals mentioned will be explained in more detail in other chapters as well.

Once the business portion of the Board meeting ends, we often move to a group healing or honoring process, depending on what is calling to us. We have some lovely ceremonies to honor birthdays either individually or collectively for those sharing birthdays that month. Occasionally, we will honor a member of the circle with a group healing for a special occasion or to assist in physical and spiritual healing when one of us is experiencing health challenges. Food and beverages may also be shared in some of the celebrations.

The closing process is another essential ritual we engage in to end the meeting. We gather in circle and often listen to a closing song and then will chant or dance, or send healing energy to those named in circle. Heartfelt hugs are typically shared by all after the closing circle ends.

The passion and loving energy generated in our gatherings is so magical and uplifting for all of us. We are held in such a palpable field of Divine love and light that it defies words and is truly an experiential phenomenon that must be felt to be fully understood. Many of us initially doubt that we truly deserve to belong to such a powerful group of alchemical healers. It truthfully is a seemingly magical process of transformation and creation that we are lovingly enfolded into when we enter the circle.

Carol Ann Robbins, PhD

Carol Ann Robbins, PhD is a clinical psychologist specializing in the diagnosis and treatment of ADHD across the lifespan. As Director of the Annapolis ADHD Center, she treats individuals of all ages, families, and couples with ADHD and co-existing disorders. Dr. Robbins is an experienced professional workshop presenter, author, and leader in her field. She brings to bear her passion for spiritual exploration, growth, and transformative healing in her work as a psycho spiritual healer. She is a student of Qigong, tai chi, and yoga and a Usui Reiki Master.

Chapter 6

Living a Multi-Dimensional Life: There's More Going on Than You Think There Is

— Reverend Rosemary Bredeson

Y ou are a multi-dimensional being, choosing to live a three-dimensional life on Planet Earth at this time.

Shocking? Hard to fathom? We've all heard that we are *spiritual beings having a human experience,* but what does that really mean?

We are simultaneously living in our regular three-dimensional world and conscious of other things going on. Have you ever had the phone ring and know who was calling before you looked at Caller ID? Have you ever felt that you should take an umbrella with you but looked at the blue sky to decide not to and, then, gotten wet?

There is something else going on.

We are able to tap into that *something else* to get guidance and information that the regular three-dimensional world isn't providing to us consciously. *This* is what it means to be aware that we are living a multi-dimensional life, whether or not we are conscious that that is what we are doing. *This* is also why it is so important to be aware of the power of what is greater than the 3-D world.

When we live from this *higher place* we are so much more powerful than if we limit ourselves to what is the so-called *reality* of the third dimension. There is a power of co-creation with the greater mind that gives us the ability to operate outside the box of what has always been, or how things have usually been done. Someday this will become the new normal in which humans will function.

When I first joined the ACT Co-Creation Council (CCC) I was already living in connection to higher consciousness and working as The Scientific Mystic, a spiritual counselor/mentor. I had learned to appreciate that the wisdom and guidance available by tuning in to higher consciousness, spirit guides, angels, the greater mind, and the higher self is where one finds better options and information than in thinking with the same consciousness that caused problems in the first place. The field of all possibilities is accessible when one reaches beyond the known world.

The first meeting that I attended was the annual retreat at the end of a program year, when the group was reviewing their year-long process of visioning the future of ACT. It quickly became apparent to me that this group didn't function the way I was used to a board of volunteers functioning!

We were invited to meditate and *tune in* to determine what role we were to play within the ACT CCC: an interesting way to choose a role. I tuned in (being a practiced meditator) and was a bit surprised that I heard that my role was to "Be The Oracle."

Now, this was my first official meeting with the ACT CCC and, although I knew most of the members, I was a newbie. It felt pretty arrogant to declare myself to be The Oracle for this group. But I followed through after the exercise and claimed my role. Surprisingly, there was no ego either in my statement of my role or in the reaction of the others. It was simply what I had received when I *tuned in*.

That was my first lesson that this co-creation thing was being practiced by a group of people who really trusted in the process of accessing higher mind and sharing what we individually and collectively received through that access. The years have only deepened my appreciation for this style of operating within a group. It works, especially when there is trust and respect on the part of every member of the group.

Collaboration doesn't have to be a competition of ideas. There doesn't have to be a battle of opposing views until one either beats the other into submission or someone sees that they are outnumbered by votes. Collaboration, in the context of co-creation through multi-dimensional living, allows each participant to tap into their internal guidance and to the higher wisdom available to the group and, in the shared experience of that higher wisdom, share a vision that can then be implemented in the three-dimensional world in which we live.

It almost seems like magic when a group of twelve people can close their eyes and access the same vision, albeit from unique perspectives, so that when they open their eyes and share what they saw, the whole picture emerges.

Imagine if no one is right and no one is wrong and everyone is sharing from a place of trusting in both the process and in the other participants. *This* is how true co-creation can be its most powerful. There is a synergy in this process that leads to the consensus sought. Egos are left at the door because everyone knows that something bigger than the individual, or even the group, is at work here. Our job is to access what that bigger vision is and then to make it happen.

Empowered Point Leadership in the Circle is shared leadership. When the entire circle is trusting in the process of accessing guidance from the greater mind, then the points around the circle can share leadership responsibilities as needed. This process doesn't mean going around and around in circles without getting anywhere! Rather, when an event or activity needs a leader, a person takes on the role of coordinator and handles that activity. When there are tasks to be done, someone takes on that task and is empowered to take care of it. The beauty of this is that everyone can be respected as a leader and everyone can also contribute on tasks, events, activities and responsibilities.

A circle does not have to stay in a two-dimensional, flat configuration. When we move into a multi-dimensional operation, we are expanding the circle to include the higher guides, the Soul of ACT or the Spirit of any organization, the angels and guides of individuals and the collective, and the greater mind at work in the Universe. The individual does not get lost in the process. Instead, the individual is valued for the part of the process that they take on as their role. The focus becomes the center of the circle, the place where all the individuals connect in shared vision. The power of the group is then magnified by this connection around the circle and into the center of the circle. The wheel begins to move.

This brings us back to *roles*. The Empowered Point Leadership model shows how honoring the roles that each person has discerned is theirs to play within the group can allow shared leadership to work. These roles are not job descriptions – they are ways to participate in the group so that agreed-upon goals can be accomplished. Again, it comes down to trusting in the process of accessing the higher guidance to determine those roles.

As The Oracle, I have spoken as I have received higher guidance in many different situations. For example, the CCC recently examined different aspects of our gatherings and the organization. We were each given a random card with a word or phrase on it. Mine was *Music and Movement*. My first reaction was to consider the great music programs that we offered throughout the year and the movement within gatherings – such as exercises to connect with others for a sharing moment or collecting in a circle for the closing ritual. But I felt there was more to it than that. As I shared with the group, I felt guided to speak about music as *vibration and frequency* and how what we offer is a high vibrational gift to attendees. Therefore, what we offer (and what we experience) happens at a frequency that supports individual and group transformation. *Movement* expanded from physical movement within the room to *starting a Movement* in the world, *being a Movement* so that ACT can lead the way for others to operate at a higher vibration with a vision to connect to transformative guidance that is evolutionary.

So what does it mean to *operate at a higher vibration*? It all comes down to energy.

Energy. Frequency. Dimensions. Oh, My! Everything is Energy. At least, that is what quantum physics is teaching us. Energy has a frequency, a vibration, a vibe, if you will. And the Universe is a place of many, countless dimensions. How do we navigate through all this?

Let's start with energy, for that is the building block of understanding that we must think of the energetics of what we are doing if we are to evolve and accomplish growth.

If everything is energy, then even our thoughts carry an energy, a vibration. It is important to pay attention to the energy of our thoughts. What is the energy around the group thought? If individuals are focusing their thoughts on making a vision become reality, their energy, and the vibration of that energy, must align with the group vision to bring that vision forward. This is where accessing a shared vision, and trusting in the other individuals as they do this, brings the energy of the group into alignment. Alignment on the same frequency creates an energetic magnet to attract what is needed to manifest the vision.

By aligning the energies to the same frequency, the group actually creates what is envisioned in a level of consciousness, another dimension, where it then exists to be manifested in the third dimension.

Think of it this way: if a group becomes so focused on supporting each other to accomplish an agreed-upon goal, then all that focused energy makes accomplishing that goal a foregone conclusion. Mental focus directs the actions of the group in the same direction.

It is all working on the multi-dimensional level, whether we are conscious of that or not. We might as well become aware so that we can consciously focus on what we do want to accomplish. Since we are always co-creating with the Universe, doesn't it make sense to focus on what we *do* want rather than what we *don't*?

If the group sits around talking about what is wrong, what they don't want, what needs to change, and doesn't bring that mental focus to what they *do* want, then the energy vibration keeps feeding what is not wanted.

It is all about the vibes.

So when you understand that reaching into the other dimensions, where possibilities exist, the dimension that holds what you want is where you want to place your attention.

Within the group, it might be one person's role to help clarify the vision, another's to help the group focus their energies, and yet another's to help to shift the fears around that vision. When the group trusts the process, each person is free to play the role that is theirs. When the whole group understands the importance of focusing the energies, the shared focus becomes easier to accomplish.

Here is the question that helps to get the focus clear.

Is this action (idea, proposal, thought) in service to:

Love? Honor? Integrity? Community? Higher Purpose?

Consensus from this perspective leads to powerful co-creation.

The role of Ritual has to be valued in all this. How does a group incorporate these ideas? How do individuals participate at this energetic level?

Every group has certain, perhaps unconscious, rituals in how they interact. There is probably an agenda for meetings, a program for events or other activities. This is not the kind of ritual we are talking about here.

There is a way for ritual to assist the conscious mind in relaxing and getting out of the way so that the higher conscious mind can be accessed. It can be as simple as taking a deep breath and focusing on relaxing. Soothing music can do this. Sometimes sitting in a particular position, or lying on the floor, can help to eliminate the worries of the day and allow the person to relax and become open and connected to the higher self.

When we talk about ritual here we are discussing the act of making sacred the space in which subsequent activities are taking place. Different religions have different rituals that they adhere to in practice. Here, we are not defining a religious kind of ritual but one that helps a group to come together to honor the sacredness of their interaction and their shared intentions. Each group will have their own rituals and there is great value in honoring the rituals that bring the individuals into group focus.

The culture of a group will direct, to some extent, the kind of rituals that are created. Shared values and beliefs help to shape those rituals. It is important that whatever is created honors and respects everyone participating.

And sometimes rituals can become shared practice organically because a group that connects, heart to heart, will want a group hug at the end of a meeting, or will adopt a song as their theme song, and will weave this into the ritual of the gatherings.

Gather is an important word here. A group with a shared intention needs to gather and connect so that that shared intention can be made manifest. Ritual works on many levels, or dimensions, to help to bring together those who would share this journey. Something as simple as sitting in a circle for the meeting and lighting a candle in the center of the circle can bring the focus to that shared intention. The purpose is the connection.

And this brings us back to multi-dimensional living. There is something greater going on here. Call it whatever term works for you, but the understanding that there is a greater mind, a force in the Universe with a plan, helps us to comprehend that we are each a part of something that is unfolding within and around us. We come together in groups to share in that unfolding.

We bring to a group all of ourselves – the baggage, the dreams, the fears, the accomplishments. We do not live in a vacuum, compartmentalizing the group member from the person outside the group. When we acknowledge ourselves as a whole person, a being who is greater than the three-dimensional physical body, then we can make our greatest contribution to any group in which we participate.

And when a group honors each member in this wholeness, then the co-creation of a gathering of multi-dimensional beings can commence!

Reverend Rosemary Bredeson

Reverend Rosemary Bredeson is The Scientific Mystic, a spiritual counselor/mentor who has been accessing higher dimensions all of her life. While working for the US National Aeronautics and Space Administration on the Hubble Space Telescope, Rosemary felt a calling to become a spiritual healer. Today she uses her multi-dimensional abilities and her training in NLP (Neuro-Linguistic Programming), Hypnosis, Reiki, etc. to help others transform their lives into the vision they dream. Visit www.TheScientificMystic.com for a *free 7-minute meditation to de-stress*!

Chapter 7

Jump Off the Circle and Enter the Spiral

—*Shannon Marie Plummer*

A t one time or another, we may have believed this life to be a linear experience where the only two guarantees are birth and death, and that everything in-between happens in a sequential time and space continuum. It is not until we mature that we recognize the circular patterns of our thoughts, beliefs, and behaviors that determine our perceptions, perspectives, and experiences. As we choose to transform and grow beyond what we believe to be our only truth in this moment, we begin to identify the triggers that invite us into the repetitive, circular experiences that create a thread of perceived suffering or confusion or victimization. We then find ourselves at a crossroad with two questions:

1. Do I make the same choice that leads me around the circle of a similar human experience again?
2. Do I make a different choice that jumps the circular course and catapults me into the desired spiral soul journey?

The spiral journey is one that encourages us to constantly observe ourselves living this complete experience of life. The movement shifts from two-dimensions to three-dimensions, highlighting dynamics that are impossible to see in a two-dimensional, circular fashion. When we open that spiral, we learn to become a witness to our own experiences, rather than getting entangled in the emotional energies of the experience itself that cause us to continue around the do-loop.

The spiral teaches us that the circular nature of life is necessary. Let's face it… the circle is still an integral part of the spiral! But the spiral allows that circle to lead us to an opening where the circle, ever so slightly, changes elevation and expands into a three-dimensional pattern. From there, we can observe upward, downward, inward, and outward motions on the spiral because our field of view changes.

Having a degree in engineering, I was keenly aware of the mathematics and the science behind circles and spirals. It was not until I began to apply the concepts in my shamanic practice that the two became a graceful dance of — nothing less than — life itself. Through my shamanic practice I was able to walk myself through the circular process on one level of the spiral, while observing myself in the same circular process on another level of the spiral. After a few times around in *observation mode*, I began to follow the threads that emerged from my own spiral of life and watched the integration with the other spirals of life around me.

One of those integrating spirals is A Community of Transformation (ACT), whose leadership team, or Co-Creation Council (CCC), is encouraged to share their spiraling life experiences in order to witness, with compassion and understanding, the spiraling dynamics of each individual's contributions to the group dynamics, both past and present.

Having served on the CCC well after ACT was an established community, I was able to listen — as the *child* — to the elders tell their stories of creation and challenges and celebrations over the years. By way of my shamanic practices, I was able to recognize both the circle and the spiral of ACT, and to identify where my personal circles and spirals might support the future of the organization.

From here we begin our journey to follow the circle until we jump into the spiral of ACT. From a shamanic perspective, the circle is represented by the Medicine Wheel, which is governed by directional archetypes and energies that guide us through every minute, every day, every week, every month, every *every* of our life.

The circle, in my tradition, begins in the South. The place where we enter the womb of the Earth. The place where healing occurs. The place where we are so fully grounded in our body that we go into the subconscious and maybe even tap into the unconscious inner depths and pull out those old stories, those limiting beliefs, those discarded concepts, and those broken dreams that are ready to be realized, with real-eyes. Why are they still there? Because there is *something* to them. There is something to be seen. There is something to be heard. There is something to be uncovered. There is something to heal. There is something to learn.

This is one quarter of the essence of ACT. A place to go inward, a place to be seen, a place to be heard, a place to uncover, a place to heal, and a place to learn — whether you attend the gatherings or are part of the CCC leadership team. The creator of ACT, Linda Roebuck, constantly encourages the CCC to, "Go within," and find the depths of what wants to be healed so that something new can be birthed. This is both in our personal — and, seemingly, individual — lives, and as the council encourages the next iteration of ACT collectively. That is what makes the energetics, or the soul, of ACT a continuous spiraling evolution. ACT is an organization that encourages members to share their healing journey with a group of others experiencing their own healing journey: without concern for the why, or how, or when, but just simply identifying and verbalizing the *what* of the journey; without judgment, or blame, or analysis, but just simply listening and supporting each other in a safe and sacred space.

The next stop on the Medicine Wheel brings us to the West: where we enter the flow of the Waters; where we find ourselves after we commit to heal the wounds of the past; where we face our fears of the present; where we allow the waters to clear our hurtful, conflicting, fearful energies and fill us with compassion and love; where we set aside the worrier energy and transform into warrior energy. The warrior who is ready to see the world with compassion and unconditional love for all who contributed — positively, negatively, and indifferently — to everything that led to the healing moment that we chose to enter in the South. Healing feels good because our heart wants us to feel our experiences and grow through them with forgiveness and gratitude for all that life brought to us. As each of us heal and face our fears internally, we up the ante for everyone around us to follow suit.

This is yet another quarter of the essence of ACT. Linda Roebuck had no idea what was in those waters when she jumped in and surrendered to its creation! ACT continually encourages each of us to jump into our own tumultuous and unknown waters, knowing there is a group of beings available to toss in a snorkel and a mask so we can breathe deeply and look below the surface, where things are crystal clear in the calm that lies below our old superficial and stormy stories. CCC members hold each other in the full potential of who we believe each other to be, which ultimately becomes a truth for us to believe ourselves. That truth helps each of us face our own fears and open to the possibilities of new ideas and perspectives that will shift the organization of ACT into a new illumination. ACT operates in the knowing that the individuals who transition in and out of the CCC leave behind their warrior energies to further develop the warrior heartbeat of ACT.

As we continue around the Medicine Wheel, we find ourselves standing in the North; standing in the whispering Wind; standing as a fearless and compassionate warrior whose core being shines brighter; standing with more compassion for ourselves, therefore able to share in more loving relationship with self and others; standing, ready to receive the messages that are deeply familiar to our spirit as the wisdom of the ages, the reminders of the ancestors; standing in our new awareness that we house these answers within and we simply need to stop, become quiet, and remember our spiritual connection (re - member, with a hyphen); standing as our own mystical awareness revealed. This revelation brings us closer to the truth of our spiritual beginning and allows us to share our sage guidance as firsthand experience, expressing and modeling as itself.

This adds the third quarter of the essence of ACT. Linda Roebuck's personal discernment process has become the staple of the organizational bylaws. The

CCC is continually asked to share what is speaking to us beyond the monkey mind language, beyond the logical answer, beyond the status quo. Call it intuition or gut feeling or mediumship or *tapping in*. What comes out is clarity of consciousness when we allow the whispers of the wind to blow through us, and the messages contained within to speak as us. Through nurturing and steady encouragement of the entire CCC, we steward our own personal connections to our spiritual support system, both seen and unseen. As the CCC sharpens that skill together, the spirit of ACT is organically connected to the wisdom of all who came before and attracts the wisdom of all who will come in the future.

To complete the Medicine Wheel and the circular healing process, we move into the East. The East brings the dawn of a new day, where our mind lights up with the passion of the Fire. The place where we see a more fully realized potential of the vision we just outgrew as we journeyed around the wheel. A vision beyond that which we could have imagined before we healed, before we rewrote our stories, before we released our fears, before we activated remembrance of our truth, before we received the advice from our wisdom keepers, before we sharpened our gaze to see far beyond the horizon. The vision that encourages us to step up, step out, and step into a new way of being that encourages complete fulfillment of this new dream, new goal, new chapter. Until we circle the wheel again, the vision continues to evolve with our own personal evolution.

This defines the final quarter of the essence of ACT. The vision. The organic and changing vision that began with a thought seed in Linda Roebuck has grown, morphed, reshaped, returned and circled the wheel with every other person who has participated as a CCC member. That ever-evolving vision continues to be fed by each individual piece of the whole. That vision drives the soul of ACT to continue and to honor the foundational healing process that created it. When we all share what we see as the future of ACT, we plant seeds for the future of ACT to sprout into being as a whole, living, breathing, evolving organization. One that honors each individual and the personal experiences they bring to the circle. One that recognizes where each person is on their own circular journey and allows each the space to ebb and flow naturally. Ultimately, each one provides a critical portion to the life force of ACT.

As each CCC member circles their own Medicine Wheel, their voices may be quieted or even silent as they enter the South, but begin to take shape as they move to the West. That is expected and supported. Their voices may be shaky as they enter the West, but are found with grace and compassion as they continue on to the North. That is expected and supported. Their voices may sound unsure and naive when entering the North, but will be filled with wisdom and sage advice by the time they head toward the East. That is accepted and supported. Their voices may express incomplete concepts as they enter the East, but will

JUMP OFF THE CIRCLE AND ENTER THE SPIRAL

emerge with a clear, full-color vision of what potential is ahead. That is expected and supported.

This is the path of the Medicine Wheel that I see mirrored in the CCC, inspired by the creative nurturing of all members who are dedicated to the Medicine Wheel of their own lives. When each of us choose to share a new, fully realized vision with the group, we step through the door into a new spiral of ACT. That spiral begins to invite and attract and magnetize the collective spirals of each individual who participates in the vision. That is what breathes more life into the soul of ACT, and that spiral activity encourages the CCC to shift and shape the future of ACT from a different vantage point. The spiral motion allows us to continue our own individual circular journeys — some that spiral inward, some that spiral outward, some that spiral downward, and some that spiral upward. As we add more and more members to the larger community, the spiral of ACT gathers energy and expands with each individual path of transformation that birthed into existence on its own.

I believe that is what Linda Roebuck, the founder of ACT, desired from the beginning: that one personal path of transformation would inspire another's path of transformation, and that path of transformation would integrate lessons of both to inspire another's path of transformation, and that path of transformation would integrate lessons of all three to inspire another's path of transformation, and so on. Thus, the spiral of ACT is born out of each individual Medicine Wheel. It is so important for humanity to honor and enter the sometimes-murky bowels of the subconscious. ACT is a way to surround ourselves — and introduce to others — a community that provides the comfort and permission for that necessary first step toward a new vision, toward a new level of the spiral, toward a new way of being. Being part of a community raises confidence and encourages everyone into a new spiral of their own transformation, knowing that each will positively affect the pool of possibilities of the larger community.

As an example, I stood in my own mud and muck, staring down the ghosts, connecting to my truth, and envisioning a change in my own personal relationship with my, now, husband, Bob Sima. Bob is not an official CCC member, though he attends all the meetings as the Music Coordinator for the ACT gatherings. Therefore, all of the CCC members knew our story in some level of understanding. They all watched our relationship sprout, develop, dismember, redefine, and remember over the six years of our courtship.

As with all meaningful relationships, Bob and I trigger each other to uncover the wounds of the past that are sleepy or dormant or pushed aside, but necessary to be healed for our own personal growth and for the evolution of our relationship together. I circled around my Medicine Wheel again and again and again, addressing the layers of healing that kept presenting for resolve. I watched as he repeatedly circled around his own Medicine Wheel doing the same. When he proposed the question of marriage, I knew that he was not only committed to his own inner work, but he was committed to supporting me as I traverse my own inner work, and vice versa. That commitment to ourselves and to each other is what allows our relationship to continually spiral into its next evolution.

What happened after he proposed was complete excitement, recognition, and support from the CCC. Not only in the celebratory nature of a wedding engagement, but in our combined dedication to the union of two three-dimensional spirals as the integration of a newly announced spiraling soul journey. The women of the CCC organized and showered me with an intentional bridal blessing of spiritual wisdom and ceremony to accompany my entry into married life. The men of the CCC coordinated an intentional evening for Bob to support his entry into married life. Many CCC members contributed their creative gifts to our wedding day.

Many CCC members were integral in the wedding ceremony. Every CCC member was glowing and always first to share a hug and a blessing and a woohoo as we consecrated our union. If ever there was a wedding rally cry, the CCC would have been heard around the world. The beauty is that they were not rallying around the fairy tale of two individuals. They were uniting as a community ready to witness and offer continued love and support to both of us through our foxholes or caverns of the South, our steady or choppy flow of the West, our gentle or stormy winds of the North, and our sparked or mature fires of the East. They were uniting to remind us that our spirals, together, are more influential than the individual spirals we each represent. They were uniting to remind us that ACT, as A Community of Transformation, was an available space to share our gifts, both individually and coupled.

As I enter the next two-dimensional evolution of my circular journey until I am ready to jump into a new three-dimensional spiral of my own transformation, I will continue to be inspired by the leadership of the CCC and the hearts of the greater ACT community, where I not only contribute and support others on their journey, but I have a place to reach out for guidance and advice on my own journey.

As you begin to recognize all the Medicine Wheel journeys of your own life and begin to identify the spiraling energy that has become familiarized as you, I challenge you to identify how an organization like ACT might support your transformation and how you could support the transformation of an organization like ACT. I invite you to invest in or help create a group or a community whose circular spirals could support a collective, journeyed path. That, in my humble opinion, is the individual circular cycle of transformation that becomes a spiraling community of transformation.

Shannon Plummer

Shannon Plummer is a shamanic practitioner and intentional creation coach. She will guide you to and through the blind spots, allowing your higher self and vision to illuminate your passion within. Shannon's intuitive and heart-centered healing, coaching, and visioning will lead you to a more authentic way of living. Her unique energy and presence creates a sacred space for expansion and deepening of what is waiting to be expressed. More at www.SpeakMyPassion.com

Part
III

Integrity: The Heart of The Process (or the Process of the Heart)

"Integrity is the courage and self-discipline to cooperate and initiate according to the Divine, which you know in your heart as Truth."

— R. Buckminster Fuller

The success of the Circular Leadership model is directly dependent on every member of the group participating from their place of heart-based integrity. They are able to sit with the question, decision, action, and more, to identify and speak their truth. They are able to define what is theirs to do and express what is theirs to share. They feel empowered to fully participate and in response feel a sense of commitment to the outcome.

The circular model and practices, as described in the previous sections, can create the space to facilitate and nourish this empowerment and commitment. But that is only half of what is needed. The individuals also need a way in which to access and bring forward their personal insights and guidance. The words intuition, discernment, and intention are used frequently in this book. They are words that are used to describe ways in which an individual can find their truth, such that they can then speak and act with integrity -- so they can be true to themselves, the process, and the group.

Integrity comes from the heart not the head. Being in integrity is not a set of *could of, would of,* and *should ofs*, but is instead a profound feeling of rightness that comes from knowing your purpose. This section contains insights, examples, and practices that are meant to enable people to connect to their own power and source of guidance — to inspire themselves and the group through direct participation from a place of personal integrity.

Chapter 8

What Does it Mean to Go Within?

—Francie Boyce

Go within? That was our instruction as we pondered how each of us could best contribute to this book. Just what does *going within* mean to me, and how did I come to my personal understanding of *going within*? Then my next question: once I *go within*, where does that take me? Am I somewhere outside myself or is there a place within that is different than what I experience on a daily basis? What should my expectations be? Should I even have an expectation? And what about intention? Where does that fit into what seems like a vague process?

I started my seeking for a meaning to this life at a very young age. I remember sitting on my bed during nap time, at about the age of two or three, wondering, *Is this it? Is this all there is?* As a young teen I read most of the spiritual books available to me in the late fifties and early sixties. My mom talked about séances, horoscopes, and psychics. She took me for my first psychic reading when I was fifteen. My notes remind me that the psychic said I would be teaching physics. At that point I had never taken physics or had an interest in the topic. I was not what I would consider a scientific person. In my fifties I started studying with Donna Eden, an amazing teacher of energy and how we can affect our own energy to evolve to a more peaceful mind and healthy body. Six years later I taught the first of what eventually became more than twelve classes a student could take to become an advanced Eden Energy Medicine practitioner. Not everyone would consider teaching energy medicine physics, especially my son who loves reading traditional physics material, but I give that psychic a thumbs up.

As a child I attended my family's church and at times felt an overwhelming sense of peace and love. Those experiences gave me the assurance that there is more than just this body and the life I was going through each day. When I was in my early forties my mom realized she could see and talk with her guardian angel. My sister would have nothing of the thought that mom could only see and talk with her own angel, and insisted that mom become a medium to allow us to have conversations with our own angels. What a gift that became for us. But still I felt dependent upon my mom for messages from *within*.

Beyond the church, my family also became involved in other methods of reaching for that feeling of inner peace. Transcendental Meditation, retreats, and group lectures became an important part of our lives. My entire family, including my husband, meditated twice a day most of our adult lives and took any available advanced classes. Our children were initiated into the practice at the age of four.

It wasn't until I met Linda Roebuck and the ACT community, whose organization stresses working in circles rather than the traditional hierarchy of leaders, that I really began to experience just what *going within* meant to me. I remember not long after Linda and I became friends that we were sitting on my pier enjoying the sun when I asked her a question. I was having difficulty deciding how to address a problem in my life. Linda's reply made a profound difference in my life then, and continues to help me today. She simply replied, "You know the answer."

I have since learned that if I pause, not worrying about what to do next, get quiet, listen and most of all trust, then an answer will come. How do I know this answer is coming from my intuition? Before answering that question, I feel a need to define just what the word *intuition* means to me. Webster's dictionary defines Intuition as, "A quick and ready insight." As I am a student of *A Course in Miracles*, I think of it as the Holy Spirit speaking to me. *A Course in Miracles* defines the Holy Spirit as the voice for God, or the part of my mind that knows the truth. So, when I go within, or listen to my intuition, I like to think of it as hearing the voice of God through the Holy Spirit, or that I am listening to that part of my mind that knows the truth. I am also comfortable with thinking of intuition as my inner guide, my guardian angel, my inner wisdom, divine guidance, universal wisdom, amazing thoughts or any other words you may use. Just for ease of writing, I will refer to all *going within* as listening to my intuition or inner guide.

It's not necessary for intuition to come as a voice in your mind. Intuition may come as a thought, feeling, urge, vision, sound or smell. We all have minds, so therefore we all have the capacity to go within and experience intuition in our own unique way. It's not even necessary to go within. Sit quietly and close your eyes to experience intuition, although at times that is very helpful. Intuition can come at any time. And the more you rely on your intuition the easier it is to access. I make it a practice to allow or welcome intuition into my daily life.

How did I start relying on my intuition? Well, first of all, when Linda told me I already knew the answer to my question I believed her. That simple reply allowed my confidence to build. Slowly I began to trust those inner messages. Sometimes what I thought was intuition was wrong, or I rejected those messages, but with practice I began to see more and more positive results from listening and trusting those messages. I started with simple things like listening to an idea about what to buy at the grocery store, or the urge to go a different route when going home. A clear example of listening to that voice when driving happened to me about ten years ago. At the last minute my daughter called to say she needed me to drive her to the airport. At that time my daughter was living a 45-minute drive from my home. After picking her up we had to back track to the airport. So, I had no time to waste. I was driving on a six-lane divided highway that usually didn't have much traffic at that time of the day. Suddenly traffic began to back up. I could see emergency lights far ahead. My first thought was that I didn't have a phone with me to alert her that I might be late, and then considered if we were stopped dead I could probably borrow a phone from another driver. Moving along slowly I had the thought to move to the center lane, which I did, trusting my intuition. But at the same time I could see the accident seemed to be in that very lane I had moved into. I thought it was strange I should move to the center lane, but I just stuck with my inner guide. As we approached the accident, the police were stopping all the cars in every lane. No one could drive forward to the clear road beyond. But the police waved me through to a clear path for there was an officer behind me who needed to get to the accident scene. I know my daughter, who just barely made her flight, was glad I listened to my intuition.

I imagine we all have had the experience of telling someone a story, seeing them listen with interest, and then get the feeling they have stopped listening. Try experimenting with a friend. One of you agrees to be the story teller and the other the listener. Agree that the listener will stop listening at some point by thinking of something else, like what you need to do later that day, or your shopping list. The listener should continue to look at the story teller as if they are still listening. Notice how long it takes the story teller to know that you are no longer listening. That's what happens to your intuition. If you don't pay attention the voice can't be heard. Worry, stress, anger, or constantly planning your life and not pausing to allow your intuition to be heard are great ways to tune out your inner guide. The other thing that can get in the way of hearing intuition is discussing and analyzing. When I go over and over in my mind just how *it* should or shouldn't be, or when in a meeting we talk and talk before making a decision, I find that then my mind has become biased. I already have decided what won't work, so as a result I'm not open to all possibilities.

How do we know its intuition? I know I'm in the flow, listening to my inner guide, and doing what is perfect for me and all others when life is easy. If I know there is a task to be done and it's a struggle to get started or complete, that's when I pause, go within, listen and trust. There is always the chance that pause will be longer than my expectation, maybe even a day or two. But I have learned to be patient, and when the time is *right* I will feel inspired, enthusiastic or happy to complete the given task. This results in a task that started out feeling like an effort becoming one that is fun and easy.

My husband and I use going in and listening to our intuition often, and as a result we no longer argue or even have conflicting desires. Here is an example of how we work. A few years ago, in the late fall, my husband wanted to buy a new car. I thought the one we had was perfect as it was only about three years old and we were both happy driving that car. He wanted a new car that had even more safety bells and whistles. He had already gone to the car dealership and together they agreed on a price that would be good until January 1st. I told my husband I really didn't see the need for a new car but would be willing to pause, go within and listen. We both agreed we would accept whatever answer I received. I had about a month to hear my answer. He was willing to give me the time I needed just as long as I knew by January 1st. I stopped and asked my inner guide (intuition). Here is an important guideline when asking guidance for an answer to a question. I start with the premise that I don't know what is best for me and others so my question must be open ended. For example, if I am on the driving trip I don't ask should I take route 70 or route 80. That limits the possibilities. Maybe there is an even better route to take, or maybe it would be best for me to stop and continue at a later date, or not go at all. If I really want to go within and hear what my intuition has to say, I should be open to all possible answers. Of course, I don't have to do what I hear and can always ask again. But I don't want to limit that inner guide. So, with the car I just asked what would be the best for both my husband and me regarding a car. Than we both had to be patient. Every week or so my husband would ask did I have an answer yet, but he remained patient. Finally, one day I was driving home in my car and, was suddenly filled with love and the possibility of the new car he wanted to buy. Our lives were saved by those bells and whistles as well as the life of a night time biker. For us it was when we were on a highway with barriers dividing the north and south bound lanes. We were on the center lane, going about seventy-five miles per hour, right next to those barriers. My husband fell asleep and the car started to drift toward the barriers. That magical car pulled us back into our lane, and, of course, woke up my husband. With the biker, my husband was driving home at night approaching a green light. Just as he was entering the cross street his car, on its own, slammed on the brakes. A biker dressed in dark clothing, with no light, rode right through the intersection. Thank you, inner guide for that car.

I've given you two very different examples of intuition. With the car I asked for advice and expected an answer. But, when I was driving to reach my daughter in time to make her flight, I didn't actually ask any question. The reason I was able to hear without asking was that once I realized I could borrow a phone and call her if needed, I relaxed and didn't worry. As a result, I was open to hearing.

Another example of listening to your intuition without thinking you have asked a question is when you have what I would describe as *those amazing thoughts*. I have found the more I take the time to listen to my inner guide the more I hear. Sometimes those messages come right out of my own mouth. I will be in a conversation, when suddenly words come out of my mouth that seem to blow me away. It's like someone other than me must have spoken those words. When did I become so wise?

So, how do I know whether what I'm hearing is my intuition, inner guide, or me just talking to myself? It's when thoughts, insights, inspirations, sensations, or feelings come, I know it's my inner guide when one or more of the following occur.

1. I'm peaceful, happy, at ease or experience any other form of joy. Fear is not present.
2. I am confident in my choice.
3. The voice or thought persists until I finally get the message.
4. The results affirm that I got the correct message, as in I bought an item that wasn't on the shopping list but it was just what we needed. Or I stopped by to see a friend just when she needed me. Or I stopped to get gas and saw that as a result I avoided getting involved in the car accident ahead.
5. Life is easy.
6. I find myself looking straight ahead with assurance that all is well and enjoy the surprises of each moment.

7. I find myself speaking and listening with amazement to the words that come from my mouth or the thoughts that appear in my mind.
8. I hear a voice with a message that brings me peace, knowing I would never have had that thought on my own.

Listening to your intuition and trusting that message makes life so much more joyful, easy, and rewarding. By *going within,* wisdom, inspiration, peace and intuition can bubble up. It works for the individual, family, group or organization. When you *go within* as a group and listen to your intuition often you will find that the majority come up with the same answer. When a group gathers with the intention of listening to their intuition there seems to be a power greater than the individual that takes over, making hearing so much easier. That is a great way to first start using your own intuition. Just relax and allow or invite the message to appear either as words, a feeling, emotion, smell, color, vision or whatever unique sensation works for you. Together our one mind has become obvious.

An example of how using intuition makes life easy happened to me this past December. I mentioned before I am a part of ACT, an organization where the governing body works in circle. In other words, we work knowing each of us has something wonderful to offer and no one is considered above or more powerful than any other. When there is a decision to be made we pause, go within, listen and trust. We were on a day retreat discussing what amazing events we wanted to bring to our community in the next months. A holiday party was mentioned. Did we want to have the same pot luck we have had for the last seven or eight years? After a short discussion we agreed to pause, go within and listen.

The idea of a catered dinner held in a venue where we would transform the room with our decorations was the result of us listening to our intuition. Then suddenly, out of my mouth, came, "I will take the lead for the party." I was so surprised by those words. I believed it would be easy and fun. Parties I love, but I have never planned and implemented such a party. Not to worry, I knew there was a voice within me that would guide me. That also meant for the first time we would charge for our holiday party. Again, we went within for guidance regarding the fee to attend our party. I so enjoyed watching just how intuition worked. One day I awoke with the idea for a spreadsheet of volunteer jobs we needed. The spreadsheet's heading was *Jobs for Fun*. As others listened to their intuition, I marveled at the fact that the perfect person signed up for each job. Knowing what kind of food to order from the caterer and how much became a worry for me. We wanted to have vegetarian, meat and gluten-free options. How much to get of each option so that everyone would have their needs met and that no one would go home hungry kept me awake at night. Then I remembered. I'm not alone. I have my inner guide, plus my friends and their inner guides.

I found a catering company that made me happy every time I spoke with them and I was confident their food offerings would be agreeable with everyone. Finally, the food and decoration orders had been set as the day for the party was fast approaching. The number of volunteers to do all the last-minute tasks seemed perfect. The morning before the party I awoke with this persistent voice that told me to order one more tray of food. This was a voice that couldn't be ignored. Of course, I heeded that voice and ordered the food. We ended up with the exact amount of food, and the exact number of helpers. Most of the decorating had to be done the day of the party. It was amazing to witness the ease at which the decorating and cleaning up after the party went. At the end of the evening I had the thought to announce that we needed to clean up, put all the tables back in their storage closet, return all the chairs to their proper location, take down the decorations and get the kitchen back in order. It was like observing locusts swarming in and taking over. Experiencing the speed, ease and fun that resulted was a great way to end this magical party that was inspired by going within, listening and trusting.

Once I began to recognize there is a part of my mind that is very wise, I have become more and more willing to trust my intuition. Not relying on what I would call the rational mind, but becoming willing to trust guidance is crucial for success. There seems to be a tipping point. As the willingness grows the answers flow and life become easier.

I recommend getting your head out of the clouds and enjoying the ease of life. What do I mean by the clouds? Imagine how it would feel if you were literally standing in a dense cloud. In such a cloud you would not be able to see your way forward or when to make a turn. You might become disoriented or confused. Time could have no meaning. When I feel as if I am stuck in a cloud of concern, worry or confusion I remember to stop, go within, listen and trust. Suddenly that cloud lifts, and the day becomes a time of ease and trust. I believe you, too, know the answer to your question. Peace be with you.

Francie Boyce

Francie has an Eden Energy Medicine practice in Maryland. She is a founding member of the Eden Energy Medicine certification program. She has taught throughout the United States and Great Britain. She can be found on the Eden Energy Medicine website www. Innersource.net/em/

Francie and her husband have been facilitating *A Course in Miracles* study group for over sixteen years. Francie's desire is to help clients and students see their own divinity within while also recognizing the divinity of others.

Chapter 9

Consensus and Discernment – Vital Practices for Circular Leadership

—Lilia Shoshanna Rae

Most of my life was spent as a lawyer for a state legislature, where Robert's Rules of Order, majority voting, and hierarchical structure were key to forming concepts into laws. One vote more than half was how legislation became law. Each legislative chamber had a leader. My department had a top boss. Authority flowed top down. Most organizations work that way. My career was steeped in it.

Midway during my career, I found myself learning and practicing a different kind of decision-making, one based on spiritual discernment practices with a goal of unification, understanding, and collaboration. I knew that governments and most groups were not ready for this kind of shift in structure and process, but it felt important for me to explore these new ways of group governing in the organizations in which I found myself. This exploration became a personal passion for me. It felt new, evolved, and expansive. I found myself searching for a place where I could feel support for my evolving spiritual beliefs. I asked three people for suggestions. They all gave me the same answer – a church behind the local bowling alley. It sounded odd. I did not know what to expect, but I could not deny that something was guiding me to this church. I mustered my courage and tried something new.

I was accustomed to churches that had steeples and windows and their own plot of land. This one had an obscure entrance that hardly distinguished it from the printing shop on one side and a beer-making supply store on the other. As I walked timidly inside, I was led to the sanctuary. I sat in the third row, not too far up front, but where I could still have a good view of the service. There was soft music playing and the lights were low, encouraging congregants to meditate before the service. I had the overwhelming sense I'd found home.

I describe this in detail because this was Spirit actively leading me to a new way of living and learning. Spirit was giving me signs I could not ignore: three random people I spoke to gave me the same answer, and this gave me a sense of home even before the first service started.

Shortly after my entrance into this new spiritual community, a group came together to hold a vision of a new location for the church - perhaps a church with windows, maybe even some grass and trees. The minister did not believe the church was ready for such a big move. She suggested we commit to a yearlong study, using a workbook titled *Rings of Empowerment* by Carolyn Anderson[1], that she had seen help groups grow spiritually into cohesive organizations that yielded transformative results. The book study required a commitment for twelve months and a willingness by each member to lead the group on one of those months.

Twelve of us made that commitment and began to meet each month. It took many years for the vision of the church to materialize, but that year laid a foundation for congregants taking responsibility for the health and welfare of the church, committing to various responsibilities, and building a framework for a more sustainable growth. A key part of that foundation was the calling of a circle, sharing leadership around the circle, and realizing that each in the circle was important.

At the core of our understanding was that each one in the circle had a role and the group needed each person to take responsibility for their role. We learned to work as a group in a new way that helped us through years of change.

After that minister left, the board of the church, in its search for a new leader, developed a practice of using consensus decision-making. While we were without a minister, it was important for the board to act as a cohesive whole. Using discernment and consensus decision-making helped the board coalesce.

This experience with the church board helped me as I served on a team developing bylaws for ACT (A Community of Transformation), a new organization, based on Linda Roebuck's vision. As part of her vision, the organization was to be co-created by more than one hundred community members who shared her vision for a holistic healing center in the Annapolis area.

Those of us working on the bylaws wanted them to reflect a new way of coming together. Consensus decision-making and discernment practices were key elements that we included in the bylaws. The formative teams were already using these practices as a part of their group processes. Through the bylaws, these tools became the formal method for decision making when it incorporated as a nonprofit corporation.

ACT's long-term success with this type of decision making can encourage other organizations that want to explore group processes that are more holistic, honoring the group as a whole.

What is Consensus Decision-making

Making decisions by consensus is a method that respects each member of the group. In its most extreme version, if one member of the group does not want to go in a particular direction, the group looks for a different outcome. The power of a single member can be much greater than most groups would allow. It can stall and stymie, even lead to group stagnation. Decision making can take longer. The whole group needs to be convinced of the value of a decision, not just the majority.

You might ask, given these possible issues, why would a group choose it as its model for decision making? What if it also led to greater group cohesion and sense of wholeness? If no one is feeling left out of a decision, would it not cause the whole group to relate differently to each other and present itself to others as a unified whole, not just a blend of competing factions?

Having seen it work for several groups, I feel it is a model more evolved for making decisions that helps the group and each individual in the group grow in consciousness.

Consensus building uses gifts of sacred geometry of the circle and triangle.

Before I was a lawyer, I was a math student. I graduated from college with a math degree and taught math at local community colleges before my work as a legislative lawyer. When I discovered sacred geometry years later, as a part of my spiritual studies, I felt a deep resonance. I thought, "This is why I studied math." It gave me the foundation for understanding the spiritual side of mathematics.

Two well-known shapes in geometry help us understand the consensus process.

First is the circle. Crucial to understanding consensus is that each person on the rim of the circle has importance. Each view is to be respected, heard, and honored as part of the process. That is why it is so important for each voice to speak up and be heard, especially from an aligned body, mind, and heart space connected to Spirit. The second geometric shape is the triangle. It represents the synthesis that occurs when a decision is made after differing points of view are spoken and heard in this aligned way.

Think of an equilateral triangle with each of the three points on the rim of a circle, with the base of the triangle connecting the bottom two points and the third point at the top.

One point of view can be called the *thesis*. Its opposite (or most divergent view in comparison) can be called its *antithesis*. So, what is that point at the top? Their *synthesis*. After each person with a different point of view has spoken and been heard, the process of synthesis, using discernment, leads to a solution based on both. Synthesis raises a conflict of ideas to a new level, or a new perspective.

This is what feels magical when using the consensus decision-making model. It uplifts the conversation of conflicting views. It allows creativity to enter the discussion. It calls on Spirit, or whatever is understood to be greater than each individual and greater than the group, to lead the group to a new perspective, and sometimes a new paradigm.

Key Elements of the Consensus Process

Here are some key elements that make the consensus process work:

- Connecting to heart energy of self, circle, and Spirit. Connecting to heart energy is so important. It is the heart energy of each member of the group, the heart energy of the group itself, and whatever the group understanding of Spirit is. Some may know that as God, the Divine, the Universe, Source, All That Is, or whatever other name or description is used by the participants. It is a power greater than any individual in the group and greater than the group.

  Sometimes maintaining this connection to heart energy requires someone in the group to call a time out. It is natural for humans to get into head energy, particularly in decision making when a certain amount of analysis and fact finding is important. The alignment of mind, body, and heart with Spirit is what makes this process work best. Our tendency is to emphasize one over the other – usually head over heart. Taking a moment to go into the quiet and intentionally restore that alignment can shift the energy of each individual and the group.

- Discernment by each member. Discernment is another vital element for the consensus process to work well. What is discernment? I call it connecting to our internal truth meter. We probably do it all the time but may not be aware that we are doing it, or may use another term for it.

Discernment is an art rather than a science. It can take practice, particularly if one is used to taking cues externally rather than internally. It requires us to realize we have an inner knower that gives us our personal truth. The clearer we sense our personal truth, the more aligned it is with that mysterious greater Truth we often represent with a capital T. The alignment process that is central to consensus decision-making helps one discern personal truth. With all of our channels for information open and flowing with each other, we can sense when something does not *feel* right, *sound* right, or *seem* right. Our mind can still function in its analytical, rational, and logical way, yet it will be using information that is not only factual, numerical, or provable, but something even greater.

- Voicing results of personal discernment even when divergent.

  One more crucial piece of the consensus puzzle that makes it work so much better is to have everyone understand and take responsibility for speaking up, when as a part of their personal discernment process, they believe a different decision, or a modification to a decision, is necessary. If someone allows their inexperience or some other excuse to get in the way of voicing their opinion when it is divergent from the rest of the group, the decision itself suffers.

Sometimes a person can go along with the group decision even when they doubt it or have a concern. In fact, we often use a signal by thumb. Thumb up is *yes*, thumb down is *no*, and thumb sideways means *I have some doubts or misgivings, but I am willing to go with the rest of the group.* Depending on the time available for discussion, the sideways signal can lead to more discussion to move in the direction of unanimity or perhaps in a direction no one considered until then. The thumbs down requires the group to stop, discuss more, discern more, but not move on in any particular direction without further exploration.

If someone does not speak up when they feel the decision is wrong, or they believe another decision would be better, the group often finds the result dissatisfactory if they move forward with that decision. As an example, early in my learning of how to use consensus, a group was deciding whether to hire someone. The search had taken a long time and many of the members were tired. The leaders of the group were especially tired. I deferred to their suggestion without speaking up out of respect and concern for them. The hiring did not work out. It was not long before another hiring process was necessary. The lesson I learned was to speak up. Even if the decision had remained the same, something could have been adjusted as part of the decision to make it more supportive for a successful hire.

Operating by Consensus Calls a Group to Work as a Whole

Consensus building allows for discussions of divergent opinions in the context of a group's intention for moving as a unified whole. It leads to decision making that incorporates the best of all opinions.

When the outlier speaks up and the group listens, amazing things can happen. Creative solutions can result that would not have been possible if the one holding a divergent view kept silent, or the group ignored them and moved on in a direction held by a majority but not the whole.

Each personality type is going to have its issues with this process. Those who like to talk are going to have to learn to listen. Those who prefer staying quiet are going to have to learn to speak up. All are going to have to learn to listen from that aligned place of mind, body, heart connection with Spirit. Aligning oneself in this way can be an evolutionary journey of its own.

I tend to be the quieter type. I have had to learn to speak up. I also had to learn to listen when I did not agree with others. As a part of ACT's board for many years, I tend to speak from the place of experience.

Experience has its place, yet it can lead to staleness and stunted growth.

One discussion that comes to mind was around membership. When you have a nonprofit organization that has a membership structure and derives part of its revenue from membership fees, it is important to have a process that works well and in sync with the activities of the organization. We found it difficult to find a process that was trouble free. One year, the newer members suggested we change the timing of the membership year. As a seasoned board member, I had seen the timing changed before. Nothing seemed to resolve the issues that kept occurring. To me, changing the membership year was just going to add confusion to the mix while not resolving anything.

I spoke up. I even held my thumb down – a very rare thing for our board. Our discussion continued. We took time to align our mind, body, and heart with Spirit in a time of quiet discernment. We each shared from that aligned, reflective space. I listened. As each spoke, I realized I was seeing things from a place of resisting change and not seeing how the proposed change made sense to the proponents. I knew that either way we were probably going to continue to have some issues, but if we made the change, at least it made more logical sense to everyone. We began our activities in the fall. Why not begin membership at the same time? After listening I could see how that made better sense. We continue to do some occasional fine tuning, yet by my listening and being able to go along with the rest of the group in making this change, we have a method that resolves the main issue of being congruent with our activities. It was important for me to speak up and to turn my thumb down. We would not have had the more considered and heartfelt discussion that we had. It was also important for me to listen – and listen from that aligned space of mind, body, heart connection with Spirit.

I feel passionately that these methods for organizational decision making by consensus, using the gifts of the circle and triangle, can lead to greater group cohesion and effectiveness. I have witnessed it in the organizations I care about the most. I know it can work for many others who are looking for ways to evolve and grow as a group and as individual members of the group.

Lilia Shoshanna Rae

After thirty years as a state legislative lawyer, Lilia Shoshanna Rae began answering her call as a messenger for the angelic realm. Lilia is the author of *The Art of Listening to Angels*[2]. She helps lightworkers and spiritual healers access angel wisdom so they can more easily and effectively live their life's purpose. Lilia is also a Reiki Master and a teacher of the Enneagram. Learn more at LiliaShoshannaRae.com.

I would like to dedicate this chapter to one of the dearest friends in my life. Zemaya Avrielle Jones birthed into Spirit on March 1, 2016. She was one of the founding members of

ACT, one of the members of the bylaws team that incorporated the consensus and discernment practices in the bylaws, and was a member of ACT's board for the first several years after its creation.

Zemaya was an inspiring force in my life helping me understand what these ideas of consensus and discernment were about. She helped me understand their transformative power. I have done my best to pass the torch. I could not have done that without her.

Notes:

1. Carolyn Anderson, *Rings of Empowerment*, Global Family, ISBN: 13: 9781883208004
2. Lilia Shoshanna Rae *The Art of Listening to Angels*, Transformational Books ISBN 9781945252143

Chapter 10

Heart-Sight: See to Create Change
—*Stephanie Sera*

How does one really learn to See? Only by seeing can truth reveal itself.

First, and arguably most difficult for many of us, is that we must become still. Notice your environment, inside and out. Relax. Now, get quiet and begin to take it all in.

Use all your senses. Look around you. Let your sense of smell take in the aroma. Now, listen to the sounds, or the silence. What does your skin tell you? Can you taste the air? Notice your feelings.

Once you utilize the five, more obvious, senses, you'll start to notice something else. As you become part of the environment, you will begin to sense something intangible… something beyond basic perception. There is an energy there. The Romans called it *Anima Loci* or the *Spirit that dwells within*. What is that presence saying? What does this energy feel like to you?

Every person and community has such a spirit, and so does every place. Learn to sense it. What is it like where you are now? To show you the difference this spirit can make, try recalling a place where you felt calm, peaceful, or truly welcomed. Now recollect an environment that felt more chaotic, disorganized, or unpleasant. How did it feel in the space you recall? How did it make you feel on the inside? This is the spirit I speak of. It's an intangible quality. Notice how you feel where you are.

This intangible quality is something that you can only see through what I call Heart-sight or *learning to see with your heart*.

When aligning myself with my own Heart-sight, I often hear Oprah Winfrey's famous line, "What I know for sure…" I ponder over that statement. It feels like a valuable place to start. What I know for sure, something that I am very practiced at, and something that I have been doing for a very long time, is to truly see. Part of this practice began when I was just a teenager taking a college course, and my dear professor, Henry Niese, would insist that every one of his students look and See.

What does this really mean? Take for instance, a tree. When asked to look at a tree in front of them and describe it, a person without the ability to Heart-See might say that the bark is brown and the leaves are green. Maybe they say this because of the way they were taught. Someone might have given that person that shorthand summation, somewhere before kindergarten, so that they would know what a *tree* looks like. That person was then conditioned from a young age so that all they could see forever after their kindergarten lesson was that every tree has a brown trunk with green leaves. This short hand description couldn't be further from the truth. In labeling things, such as a tree, with short hand characteristics such as brown bark and green leaves, we develop a mental image of the thing and stop seeing it for what it is. This shorthand labeling serves a purpose in childhood: it helps children quickly log information in a world so full of things they need to understand that they could easily become overwhelmed. But there is a cost to this shorthand and rapid learning: they stop Seeing with their hearts. As a child ages, there is a pronounced shift in the way that child describes the world and the many entities within it. As we become thoughtful adults, we would be wise to seek out those initial impressions the world has on our senses and ruminate on the way it affects our emotions and energy.

Someone without the Heart-Sight will say the tree has brown bark. But, really, how many colors exist in that bark and what are the undertones? The time of day, seasons, the quality of light, among countless other factors, are constantly changing. This alone affects the coloration. To Heart-See, look at the texture of the bark. Is it smooth or rough? And these leaves, so simply described as green: are the leaves transparent or opaque? Can we see the veins? What patterns form those veins?

Does this pattern complement other aspects of this tree we're seeing?

One day when I was looking closely at a tree, I began to see patterns. The fractals and intelligence of it all were overwhelming. I looked around to the combination of surrounding plants, to their relationship to the tree, to one another, and to me. I became aware of the colonies or drifts of certain species. The clusters wove into each other like a tapestry. It was beautiful to bear witness to this. What came through my eyes found its way into my heart. By observing all that was around me I became part of the experience myself.

Professor Niese would tell us to look at a tree, and ask us what we saw. He insisted that we see it as if for the first time for what it truly was. As artists, most of us thought we already did this, but that day I connected to something deeper than just the colors. Maybe he knew how important learning to See really was. Maybe he knew that as we transitioned into adulthood, we would stop Seeing with the innocence and clarity of childhood—the childhood before we learned that the *right* way to see a tree was as something with brown bark and green leaves. He knew that our minds would soon obscure our true vision or sight. I think he honed a quality in me right before it could be extinguished. His exercises made an indelible impression on me and helped me maintain my childhood ability to See.

It's not too late. You can learn it, too. By learning to see, you can even add something new to what is there in front of you. You can begin to compose or create. For example, once an artist can see, they can edit power lines from a landscape or a blemish from someone's face. One learns to choose the best angles for the subject and even to change colors if need be. Once a person truly Sees, they can take certain liberties with their creation. The same thing works in your life.

My work today is to use my skills of Heart-Sight to make people's surroundings beautiful. I'm a Designer. My earlier training allows me to see the common threads in people's environments, as well as aspects of themselves that have transferred into their surroundings. Not only do I see what is there at the start of my work, but I also I see how everything can come together in harmony, including what needs to be moved or removed. I'm directed by an inner knowing, an intention, to bring all these different elements together in the best way possible. Seeing opens up the possibilities of what may come and allows me to see the potential of one piece beyond its current state and envision it in a new light.

When you work together in a group, there are many threads to weave, as well. To bring everything and everyone together in harmony, you must honor the role of your heart.

Heart and mind are both important: for instance, I think my mind helps me to sort out all the pertinent information as I work, but it is in my heart that things are transformed and woven together in a coherent way. Heart is what brings it all together.

Heart? What does heart mean? To some, this energy of harmony that I tap into is simply evidence that I've become accomplished at my trade as a designer. But it's more than that. There needs to be a love for the work, but it must stand on its own. Heart pays respect to all of the elements and makes it possible to show them in their best light. In Circular Leadership, this is the energy of honoring every member in the space.

Even if the spirit of a space is in chaos or discord, it can be adjusted, probably just as any individual or group can, too. As I've learned, our environments can affect us as well as reflect what's going on within us. Group dynamics can relate to what is going on inside of us as individuals. Fortunately, we have the ability, and the power, to do something about it. As we each lovingly clean up our space, and rearrange things in their best light, we bring a sense of harmony to it and to ourselves. The work that you do for your own space will spread to others around you.

In creating a new vibe to a space, you can be playful, of course, and make joyful combinations of elements like adding delightful pops of color. Whatever you create will reflect back to you. For most, if you create calm, you will feel calm, and if you want to pump up the volume you will feel energized. However, everyone is different. For instance, a calm environment recharges my batteries while riotous color winds up depleting me. Learn to see in a multi-sensory way and you will understand these sorts of distinctions about yourself.

Do this exercise: tap into your personal spaces. They are metaphors for what is going on within you. You don't need to judge yourself; this is about simply asking the questions. Do this now if you are at home, or do this as soon as you get a chance. To begin the exercise, take a breath. When you tune into a space around you, what is being reflected back to you? Are you feeling any certain way—are you feeling hurried, and do you lack the time to put things away? Have you experienced a loss that is paralyzing you or making you hoard stuff? Do you keep communal spaces tidy, yet neglect your personal bedrooms? Are your closets filled with memories of another time? Or is your place cold and unwelcoming because you aren't fully present there? Look at it all with compassion and love. Begin where your heart leads you.

As within, so without. It's all a feedback loop, so start with either the inside (self-care), or begin with the physical space that's around you. It all connects. By adding, subtracting, or rearranging you will begin to change it and improve it to your liking. Tend to your spaces, inside and out, and the results will ripple into the spirit of your community environment, too.

It is said, one cannot solve a problem with the same energy that created it. Yet with this newfound way of seeing with your heart, you can make a change to the problems you face alone, or together. Start to learn the lessons of Professor Niese and see things poetically. When you can see the beauty of a weed growing in between rocks, then you are seeing with your heart.

The weed's determination to survive touches our heart; we can identify with the weed. We know what it feels like to be that weed, and we know that if a little weed like that can blossom in the harshest of circumstances, we can as well.

You can use this same approach to tend environments out in the world. Everything gives back in direct proportion to how much you put into it. My hope is that we all become good stewards, take care of our parcels of land or the pots on our balconies with love, and the plants and the wildlife will respond.

We may not have the power to change the world in a flash, but I believe how we *see* can make a difference in how we care for the world, for others, for ourselves, and for our possessions.

As we work in our inner and outer worlds, we contribute to All. We contribute to a spirit greater than us, and we can contribute to our groups and communities. A gentle reminder is that I feel we are guided to do this out of reverence for All Life. Deep down inside all of us is the desire to be in harmony with that source.

We can see humanity in others with our Heart-Sight. Where you once were not able to see past someone's external appearances or superficial qualities, look deeper. Perhaps you made some mental assumptions, just like people tend to label a tree and only see it the most basic way. Use all your senses and feelings as you pay attention to others: you can get the impression of the chaos or harmony that lies within, and the energy that emanates from their being. If you tap into your Heart-Space and get centered, you can often have a positive influence on your fellow man.

Let us choose coherence in our hearts and minds so that we may radiate this healing presence. See everyone whole, healed, happy, and at peace, and it is so. This is Heart-Seeing.

Stephanie Sera

Stephanie Sera is a citizen of the world, who lives in Davidsonville, Maryland, where she runs a small design business. She is married to her husband of nearly 40 years, is the mother to four children, with one grandchild and two dogs. She enjoys practicing Reiki, gardening, and cooking. Her greatest desire is to come full circle and return to the world of painting.

Chapter 11

Giving Up Membership in the Flat World Society

—Gloria Hesseloff

I am inviting you to go on a brief journey to get an idea about the exciting and profound times we are living in at this auspicious moment. Imagine, just imagine, it is the late 15th century and you are Christopher Columbus. You have been frustrated trying to get the funding for your grand idea to sail west until you reached Asia (the Indies) to find the riches of spices, gold and pearls. Even though this could be a truly profitable venture, there was huge resistance to this concept because everybody absolutely knew the world was flat and Columbus' plan would be a disaster as the ships would certainly fall off the earth. Period.

Finally, Queen Isabella's decision to take the leap to fund the program changed everything that people thought about the world and life itself! It challenged many of humanity's most cherished beliefs.

Notice the phrase above that Queen Isabella *took the leap* to see life in a different way, and it deeply changed our ideas about *the very nature of reality.* They say history repeats itself, and in the early part of the 21st century, we are once again being summoned to take a quantum leap into a new paradigm. Our present test is to update the map of life on Earth again, this time not the geographical map, but an updated psycho-spiritual map profoundly supported by the new sciences. We are so much more than we perceive ourselves to be. As an evolutionary astrologer I believe this is an extraordinary time on Earth, although it can feel so confusing and frightening. I like to think of it as a time for remembering who I really am as a vital piece of the Divine, and we are being given an incredible opportunity to consciously participate in the evolution of life on Earth. This is cause for celebration!

It's our time to join the ranks of transformers like Columbus, Queen Isabella, Galileo, Copernicus and many other brilliant and brave paradigm busters as we embrace the world of co-creation through intention setting. So many of us have spent decades evolving into higher states of consciousness and have taken great leaps in that direction. We know we are being propelled into a state of enlightenment and still have more transformative work to become the potent and refined people we know we can be. We are *a work in progress.*

As I resign from that Flat World Society, along with the rest of us, there is a need for an updated and lovingly prepared guidebook explaining the next evolutionary steps in human transformation. We are the masters of our physical reality and we have much influence in how we recreate our world. This guidebook needs to illuminate the scientifically proven capabilities of the human race of this century. I believe this anthology can make a worthy contribution to this effort, through a heartfelt vibration shared by the readers, the writers and the Divine.

We are being shown the nature of our extraordinary human capacity! The Aquarian Age we are preparing for is all about our expanding human potential. Sounds so exciting! When we open our hearts and minds to our expanded human potential it can make the present chaotic world feel less overwhelming. Perhaps we can begin to see a truly valuable purpose in our old crumbling institutions. Do any of us really want to see the world remain as it is now? Let's dive into this new paradigm that is encouraging and challenging us to grow into our Higher Selves, a path to grace and enlightenment.

Indeed, intention setting is empowering as we continue to participate in *consciously* creating our lives. Doesn't that concept move us along the path from the limiting familiar world to a remarkable new way of living? Imagine feeling more in charge of your life.

Frankly, I love the feeling of being the author/authority of my world. When I began writing this chapter I was feeling intimidated by the responsibility of sharing my experiences with manifestation through intention setting. I was stressing too hard and felt that familiar ache in my shoulders. However, my overwhelming passion for this subject kicked in and I said to myself, "Gloria, you have been dubbed 'The Goddess of Good Times'. Live up to that noble title. Lighten up! How can I reclaim my power?" I thought, Oh my gosh! Here I am writing about intention setting, which is one of the most effective and efficient methods I know, and I quickly proceeded to write this intention for both the readers and myself.

I AM so grateful and blissful that this chapter has been a flowing expansive, fruitful, and empowering experience for the readers and for me. (It is absolutely vital to focus on the heartfelt feeling I chose (bliss) as I state my intention. More about this later...)

It worked! I find myself wanting to dance with joy because the words are just flowing onto the pages. I visualize that you, the participants are actually having a heartfelt experience reading this chapter and this anthology as expansive, fruitful, and empowering. Bless our hearts, together we are truly moving to a new frontier! I visualize us all gracefully entering this exciting new reality of owning our precious rediscovered gift of being creators of our world. Thank goodness, those who have gone before us have given us some worthy rules to follow.

The above intention is the present result of the evolutionary process I embarked on about thirty-nine years ago, when I first learned about setting intentions, which were then called *affirmations*. I have seen my writing of intentions evolve every few years through the process of research and my own gut feeling of what is good for me. This is how I am working with intention setting now and I love it, but each of us needs to find our own way of doing this personal work. I trust our intention setting will continue to evolve, because that is really what this lifetime is about ... evolving.

These are the guidelines/processes/procedures/ rules/systems I use right now.

(Can't wait to see what I will be doing in three years).

- State your intention as if it has already happened and is already yours.

  We create our lives with our thoughts. Figure out what that desired life would look and feel like. Then set intentions as if that life already existed. The mind doesn't know the difference between a memory, a dream, or reality. So, if the brain thinks what we are intending is real, it will build or strengthen neural pathways that become our normal. It can be the default we naturally come to in our daily lives.

- We live in Fields of Probability.
The future contains many possibilities. We unwisely become devoted to what we perceive as *the* reality rather than what is really only one choice of several! My brilliant, evolutionary astrology teacher and mentor, Steven Forrest, refers to this when he teaches the concept that in the future stretches not fate, but a tangled web of probability curves waiting to be tested, chosen and shaped. The future is not predetermined. By using our free will and intention setting we have the ability to bend those probability curves in our favor.

- Combine a clear intention and *elevated emotions*.
This is how one of our generation's paradigm busters, Joe Dispenza, describes his process in his life-changing book, *Becoming Supernatural*[1]. Those thoughts, which make up our intention, are the electrical charge we are sending out into the unified field. In the past I might have said, "I am intending that my workshop is a success for the participants and me." The results of my intentions really improved when I came to understand these new concepts. When I combine my intention with an elevated emotion, such as love, gratitude, inspiration, joy, excitement, bliss and even ecstasy, I see stronger results. Now I focus on getting myself into that delightful high emotional state

that I would feel when that precious intention actually manifests. I ask myself, "How would I really feel if my workshop was a great success for the participants and me?"

Then I get into a chosen good feeling, focusing on making the expected emotion be a vibrational match to my intention. So, while my wording may be somewhat different, "I am joyfully intending that my workshop is a success for the participants and me," what is really significant is that my heart seems to expand with that positive feeling and I sense my energy field is far more potent. The way I understand it is we need to develop an electromagnetic field to create our intention. The electric charge is the intention. The elevated emotion, with its higher energy, is the magnetic charge we are sending out to the field. (The Goddess of Good Times just loves the idea that she is a *magnetic* being and so are you.) Dispenza refers to these elevated emotions as heartfelt. The more elevated the emotion you feel, the more influence you have on the material world of matter. An added benefit is that I am focusing on blissful emotions so much more often throughout the normal day when I use this technique, and that adds to my daily happiness. Whoever thought evolving could be so much fun!

- Make *gratitude* an important part of your intention setting.

  I have become familiar with the potent energies associated with words such as gratitude, appreciation and thankful. I am deeply thankful I can select a new reality to enhance my life and world. Gratitude is one of the strongest forms of *receivership*. I more readily receive what I desire when I am in a state of appreciation. Again, here is another unexpected benefit to my intention setting practice. I am injecting a state of gratitude into my daily life and I feel as if it is propelling me toward a greater state of enlightenment.

- Intention Setting has become a Spiritual experience for me.

  One of the most precious concepts I have gotten from astrology is the understanding that the cosmos is ensouled and this soul is known as *anima mundi*. This enchanting view leads to the idea that our human psyche is implanted in a world soul where we are part of the cosmos and the cosmos is part of us. The concept that we live in a meaningful universe empowered me to be the author of my reality through intention setting. Often, as I generate my intentions, I get a mystical sense that perhaps the cosmos is actually being expressed through me. I want to nurture this noble notion, which takes the act of creation to a whole new level.

Let's go way, way back in history as we discover that the very first intention was, "Let there be Light," and that worked out pretty well! That intention came from Source, and we came from Source, thus the world of shamanism refers to some of us as sorcerers! It is amazing to realize that the world was *intended into being by the Divine*. We can't get more spiritual than that. This realization kept me on the path of creation, gingerly following in the steps of The Creator and acknowledging the importance of modeling myself after this true Source of creativity. Honoring my inner divinity is my most cherished gift, and that has guided me to reclaim both power and beauty back into my world. Manifestation through intention setting is a major force here. We are so much more than we think we are.

Let's again look at that original intention, "Let there be Light." Another way The Goddess of Good Times likes to look at that is to "Lighten up already!" To quote H.L Mencken (but often attributed to Voltaire), "God is a comedian playing to an audience that is too afraid to laugh." With that, I would like to share a hilarious true story that happened when our group, A Community of Transformation (ACT), had a board meeting. As usual, we sat in a circle and our wise leader Linda Roebuck suggested we set an intention for a large upcoming workshop. Members proposed many wonderful ideas for that intention. Since we had taken the leap and rented a very large venue we wanted a large turnout for the program. I chimed in and suggested the idea that we visualize, "the hordes are coming." While most members liked this idea, one puzzled looking member asked, "Gloria, why would you say 'the whores are coming?'" That was over ten years ago and we still love telling that story. It lightens us up. Humor, fun, and pleasure are part of setting intentions! By the way, the "hordes" did attend that day.

• *In setting an intention be specific...or be open-ended?* This issue has been perplexing for me and, again, reminds me that I am a work in progress. I guess that is what evolving is all about. Numerous research studies have shown that being very specific about what you want to manifest works quite well when setting your intention. The more specific the better. The researchers are very adamant about this point. Years ago, I followed this way of being and it worked well for me. However, as I developed a closer relationship with the Divine, I began to question this method. I know just what I want, but is that coming from my higher self? Is it ego based? From my human, limited self, will I be limiting the good that only God knows? For now, I prefer to be more general in setting my intention. I just use the word *thrive* and know that Source best knows the truth and specifics of what is for the highest good in a particular situation. This has been working well for me. I am amazed and pleased, that for now, I will stay with the more general intention of calling for *thriving*. However, to cover my bases, I am now adding the phrase at the end… *"I am invoking this, or something even better."*

Now let's delve into how I weave these newer techniques into the evolved intention I use now.

"I AM so grateful that this chapter has been a flowing expansive, fruitful, and empowering experience for the readers and me."

(It is absolutely vital to focus on the heartfelt emotion that would be a vibrational match to how I would actually feel when the intention is materialized. I asked myself how I would really feel then and I chose to get into a feeling of Bliss as I stated this particular intention).

1. I begin with I AM, which for me represents the Spiritual aspect of the I AM Presence of God. Some of my clients or class participants choose not to begin with I AM. That is fine, because each of us must find our own path on this grand venture. It helps me get into a vibrational match with my intention.

2. Then I include the heartfelt feeling of being blissful, because I believe that is how I would feel when my intention manifests. It is absolutely fundamental to deeply experience the high emotion that helps us become a vibrational match to our desired result.

Asking yourself how you would feel if your intention was fulfilled is a helpful way to select the emotion to focus on.

3. I use the word grateful, thankful, or appreciative. Gratitude is one of the strongest forms of *receivership*. And I want to receive my good. Often, when I get into a high joy vibration, I get really enthusiastic and use all the gratitude synonyms I know. Sometimes I like to look in the mirror after doing this, and I always have such a great smile on my face and my eyes are sparkling.

"I AM grateful that the readers and I are thriving through the process of experiencing this anthology. I am invoking that this or something even better has manifested."

If I wanted to be more specific I might write something like this:

"I AM so grateful and blissful that this chapter has been an expansive, fruitful, and empowering experience for the readers and me. The words came to me easily. My concepts were well organized. I AM so thankful that the emotions I felt were a vibrational match to my goals. I AM appreciative that the readers received so much out of this chapter and the whole anthology. This book was a life enhancing experience for them. This, or something even better, has manifested for the writers and readers of this anthology." (*Remember to use all of your five senses while experiencing your intentions.*)

Intention is indeed an extraordinary force in the universe. When you think about it, all things that occur in this world are the result of intention! This force, like everything else on Earth, is continually evolving. Living in this ensouled cosmos, I am fascinated by the changing face of manifestation and intention setting at the new frontier of the 2,000-year Age of Aquarius. As an astrologer I have been observing these transformations in relation to Aquarius, the sign of groups, altruism, freedom and new ways of living.

The time of Group Consciousness is upon us. Synchronistically, this is beginning to introduce us to yet another way to create empowering intentions. The basic concept is to form a group of people and choose one person to be the receiver of the groups' intention. The members develop a sacred relationship with not only the receiver but also with each participant, as the group merges together becoming a powerful super group. Some describe it as a holy encounter. Study after study has shown the truly successful results for the receiver of this experience. However, the compelling surprise of these studies is that the group intenders have unexpected and impressive healings of their own, as a result of participating in this altruistic group! One of the descriptions I have heard for the meaning of the Aquarian Age is, "What is good for all of us." What a beautiful intention for our anima mundi as we invite enchantment back into our lives.

As we enter the Age of Aquarius we are leaving the 2,000-year-old Age of Pisces. The higher level of this era was universal love and compassion. The lower energy was victimhood. The Aquarian concept of being challenged to leave behind the victim/martyr mentality profoundly impacts *successful* intention setting. Many have been perplexed why they have trouble producing fruitful results with manifesting their desires. Instead of blaming the process of intention setting, wouldn't it be more productive to ask yourself, "What part am I playing in this stubborn situation?" After working with clients for many years, I concluded that one of the most persistent obstacles to desired results is that outworn, insidious Piscean concept of "The unworthiness of victimhood." How can we be a vibrational match to a splendid intention when we just do not believe we deserve the very good we are invoking!

In conclusion, I personally have found the practice of manifestation through intention setting to be a valuable part of my spiritual life. I have an encompassing, sweet longing to grow as a Soul. That spark of desire to evolve is nurtured as I work with intention setting, cultivating it and feeling it grow in my heart. Whoever thought evolving could be so pleasurable!

Let there be Light.

Gloria Hesseloff
Gloria Hesseloff holds a Masters degree in Education, is a certified counselor and an astrologer and the "uncertified" Goddess of Good Times. She is a metaphysician who integrates the new sciences of quantum physics and neurobiology with her astrological passion. Gloria has been on the Co-Creation Council of ACT for eighteen years and the Program Chair for seventeen years, helping advance ACT's unique mission to do collaborative good in the community and the world.

1. Joe Dispenza, *Becoming Supernatural*, Hay House, ISBN: 9781401953119

Part
IV

The Commitment to the Individual

"We can never obtain peace in the outer world until we make peace with ourselves."

—Dalai Lama

It is often said that a chain is only as strong as its weakest link. While that might be true, it turns out the circle is as weak as its strongest member. This phenomenon is a product of many different truths regarding energy, alignment, vibration, and oneness.

Self-work leads to self-understanding and self-acceptance, which in turn leads to self-worth. Self-worth is a core requirement for self-love – one cannot give or accept love if they do not feel worthy. Many of the authors reference the quote usually attributed to Mahatma Gandhi about, "being the change you want to see in the world." There is an implication that one must focus on the self to be able to make things better for others: that they need to put on their oxygen mask first in a time of crisis or need.

The potential of the circle is dependent on the personal power demonstrated by the individuals who make up that circle. If that circle is to lead and innovate, then the individuals must continue to develop themselves in a manner that will enable the identification of new ideas, opportunities, paths, or capabilities. The authors in this section share personal stories, highlighting the transformation that can occur when the journeys of the individuals are supported by the circle. The integrity of the circle then increases in strength and potential as the individuals engage from their new place of power.

Chapter 12

Living the Questions:
Living the Quest
—*Marilyn Apirian*

Who can understand the great call to the sacred work of one's life? What causes some to awaken from their family, and culturally-formed, adaptive lives and begin to respond to a more soul-directed, unfolding expression of the life force within themselves? What calls some to forgo the safety of living in the domain of the known world and, instead, to choose the unmapped and risk-filled adventure towards a destiny that mysteriously beckons?

This Sacred Call to embrace life in its fullness is evident everywhere in the natural world. Acorns are thickly sprinkled over the forest floor near my home. Yet only a few will experience conditions ideal enough to awaken them out of dormancy. Even for these, the first evidence of this occurs out of sight, within the safe womb of the earth, wherein the seed develops a root system, as it sends forth a shoot, which in time breaks the boundary of the earth's floor and begins to live into a new expression of itself. The long journey from germination into the mature expression of its internal blueprint requires the plant to be continually nurtured by environmental conditions and to endure and successfully adapt to environmental challenges.

All humans carry within themselves the blueprint of the Sacred Expression of their unique selves. Each is born with the light of their essential nature apparent in her eyes and energy field. Given this, the human experience at its most profound level is forgetting this sacred essence upon birth and, then, choosing whether or not to respond to the Call of Life, to remember and to follow trustingly where that leads. Like seeds, for a human to grow into physical maturity they too must be nurtured and endure unfavorable conditions. This particularly applies to soul and spiritual growth and maturity.

This is my story of awakening, and the understanding I have derived regarding the opportunities for spiritual transformation and following one's personal calling. As is often the case in journeys of self-awakening, the beginning starts with a couple of endings. The end of my marriage, coupled with my sister's death, catapulted me into foreign territory and I crawled into therapy. And so began my personal quest: *Who am I now, and what do*

I do now? Only later did I inquire: *What is my life about? What must I let go of? What must I welcome in? What am I being called to?*

Fast forward eighteen months - I was the head of a household of two young children, unemployed and struggling financially, when I was offered a life-line. This came in the form of a job, working as a technical editor at the Electromagnetic Analysis Center for the Department of Defense. This mathematical and scientific research center used computer analysis to model the effectiveness of the frequency spectrum of transmitters and receivers, taking into consideration interference from nearby communications equipment, atmospheric conditions, land structures, etc. Armed with a BA degree and eight years of volunteer experience, with the support of people within and outside of this organization, and with the determination to make the most of this opportunity, I set about mastering a whole new domain, eventually obtaining an MS in Computer Science and working successfully as a software development team leader.

Fifteen years later, the questions started to change and so did the answers. In recognition of a powerful Inner Call, I left the financial security and status of this career to return to school to master a whole new domain of service, more closely aligned with my core values, gifts and interests. Subsequently, as a licensed social work counselor, I began thirteen years of serving hospice patients and their families through the challenge of dying and death. As a yoga and meditation practitioner and teacher, I had become sensitive to the human electromagnetic field and the frequencies emitted, my own and others', varying with the mental, emotional, and spiritual state of the individual.

As part of a team in a hospice, my focus was to offer pyscho-social and spiritual support, resources, and processes to assist patients and families in navigating this unmapped experience in their lives. Participating in this manner provided insight into the different ways in which people move through the questions raised for them during this time of transition. While some endured stoically, or fearfully, what was happening to them, others allowed themselves to embrace the sacred healing and wholeness paradoxically accompanying this approaching experience of loss. This continuum of choice and vision could be sensed in the electromagnetic fields and in the energetic *feel* of the individuals, of their home, and within their relationships.

Early in my hospice experience, while compassionately connecting with a sleeping dying man, energy began spontaneously flowing from my hands into his body. Consequently, I trained in Reiki and began to consciously offer this energetic support as a volunteer within the hospice. By honoring this new step on my path, I was able to engage more meaningfully with those I was serving and in return they provided me insights that shaped my next steps. During the deep listening I offered to the dying, they began to describe for me how, "the veil between worlds," parted so that they were in "all time."

They could see and communicate with loved ones and spiritual beings who surrounded them and who prepared them for their transitions. These patients exhibited a perceptible energetic radiance, even as they dealt with the physically challenging realities of the dying process. Years later, arriving by the side of my daughter's dead body, my eyes were mysteriously opened and I saw her light body lying over her inert body. From that moment on, I was increasingly aware that I was living in two worlds, that of the secular and that of the Mystery, and my abilities to sense and communicate with this world have increasingly grown. I had moved past *Who am I now?* and *What do I do now?* I had been navigating *What is my life about?* and *What must I let go of?* I was now actively working with *What must I welcome in?* and *What am I being called to?*

In time I was led to engage in extensive training in shamanic medicine, working with Peruvian and Ecuadorian shamans as well as contemporary shamans in the United States. As the wisdom teachings of these ancient traditions convey, as my own healing and awakening has revealed, and as my work facilitating this healing with others over the past decade has reinforced, we have within us the potential to grow into a higher-frequency, radiant light body within this life time. The big questions that engage me now focus on why and how we humans may grow into light-filled and light-emitting beings, using the raw material of our life experiences to create *The Great Work of Your Life*[1], as the senior yogic scholar Stephen Cope describes and names it in his book, and from this unique unfolding participate with others in creating a new possibility for our shared lives on the earth.

For many, the first stirrings towards awakening are unconscious. Experiences and people begin to subtly loosen a person's *buy-in* to her outer-adaptive identity and charted path. Fidelity to an outer-directed life softens and an increasing commitment to trusting her own inner directives emerges. An unwelcomed event, like my marriage's end and sister's death, may force a break with the known world and beckon her into conscious awakening. If the person, recognizing the Grace in her life (whatever the pain), allows herself to value the new sense of Self and to feel the new freedom and possibilities arising within herself, she may overcome the temptation to deny, disregard, or rationalize away The Call and chose to accept being the co-creator of her own life, embrace risk, and pursue her own becoming.

The renowned mythologist, Joseph Campbell[2], identifies this adventure of conscious growth as, "the hero's journey." It is an epic undertaking because to accept The Call is to experience vulnerability, confusion, and fear, which have typically been repressed and denied in order to navigate the outer world with approval. It requires accepting unimaginable threats to one's identity and security, including Self-sabotaging personality and behavioral patterns. It requires full ownership of life choices, made in fulfilling outer expectations, and of the consequences. It requires learning and implementing new strategies for living in integrity with one's Inner Self. It requires becoming intimately aware of the circumstances and people who have been instrumental in one's unconscious development, and of those resources and people who can support you as you redirect your life with these new insights, new dreams and new potentialities – as you now begin the crafting of your own Sacred Life.

This commitment to self-examination, facing the demons and welcoming back denied parts of one's Self, is a way of increasingly living into the sacred expression of one's unique Self. It is experienced as greater freedom, integrity, and aliveness – as a coming home. It can be measured in an increase in the individual's electromagnetic vibration. As the individual who integrates the new gifts and awareness into her life, contributes to the life-honoring evolution of the human community and of the cosmos.

This transforming work is not a one-time effort. Alert, the individual recognizes the reoccurring call to let die yet another aspect of cherished belief (illusion about himself and the way things should work) and to birth himself again. Refusal of the call is always the easier way. To be a transformational leader and to carry any authority for mentoring another, a person must actively look for and embrace opportunities for greater consciousness and empowerment. He has learned to perceive obstacles as *miracles in disguise*. Even as he consciously surrenders to the pain of dismemberment of his old self, he draws on inner resources of compassion, courage, and trust in a benevolent purposeful Higher Power. As he anticipates the soul and spirit gifts and growth that these experiences reliably bring, this way of living is a willing surrender to the Great Call of the Universal Life Force to live into the Sacred Work of One's Life.

Why is this process essential to understand in mentoring others? Why is this essential to understand in intentionally formed groups?

The *hero's journey* has long been realized at the individual level. To serve the evolution of human and cosmic consciousness, we are called to join our energies together with others. This epic way of living leads *the transformed and always transforming* person to want to mentor others on their journeys. This intentional way of *walking the talk into ever greater consciousness* is essential for all counselors and healers. The deep knowing from which a mentor speaks cannot be developed or accessed from the rational outer-world self-oriented mind, because this mind is shallow, rooted in the world of hubris. This deep knowing can only be developed and accessed by the Heart-and-Mystery-rooted Mind-Self; this Inner Rootedness is continually referenced for guidance by the humbly conscious mind because it knows that *it does not know what it does not know.*

This epic way of growth is likewise essential for groups whose purpose is to respond to the Great Call of the Universal Life Force to live into the Sacred Work of Its Life – to mentor the evolution of the human galactic soul and spirit. The group must learn to confront and work through obstacles. The group's safety and equanimity must be risked in order to respond to and resolve unconscious blocks that threaten the group's soul and spiritual force. This requires each individual's attunement to her own inner reactivity and the courage to bring this to the group's attention. This requires a process for expecting and welcoming these flags as *miracles in disguise* and for navigating this unknown territory within the group's life. This process is most successful if it is recognized – and even role-played - at the group's inception. It recognizes and celebrates the unique and differing gifts and perspectives of its members that will lead to differences and a journey into the unknown and to new discoveries, all of which will feed its evolution.

Let us – individually and with others – do the sacred work of becoming clear transmitters and receivers of the Oneness. We must identify and address the interfering sources within and outside of ourselves. Let us become Sacred Instruments of the Holy in service to the evolution of human and cosmic consciousness.

Marilyn Apirian

Marilyn's background includes software engineering, counseling and hospice social work. She has taught yoga and facilitated energy healing using a variety of modalities for over twenty-five years. She prefers to use experiential processes to assist participants in discovering their own insights and truths and to determine their next steps for integrating these into their lives. Marilyn's personal focus is compassionately pursuing her and other's evolution into what Peruvian shamans have foreseen -- into *homo luminous*. Email: marilynapirian@gmail.com.

Notes:
1. Stephen Cope, The Great Work of Your Life: A Guide for the Journey to Your True Calling, Bantam Books, ISBN: 9780553807516
2. Joseph Campbell, The Hero with a Thousand Faces, The Collective Works of Joseph Campbell, Bollingen Foundation, ISBN: 9781577315933

Chapter 13

From One to All

—Karen Brachman

My absolute knowing of the sacredness of all life and my powerful connection to a higher source was puzzling until I realized that my near-death experience as an infant might have given me these insights and knowing. I do not have visual memories, but I have a deep knowing and understanding of certain Truths. Helping is what makes me happy. That is who I came here to be. I know I can make things better.

I knew … and then I forgot. The experiences and circumstances of our lives provide pivotal moments when our identity and personality, our beliefs and behaviors solidify. I easily slipped down the well-worn path toward duality.

Neither of my parents grew past their childhood traumas. My mother was depressed and afraid. She lived in the shame and guilt of being unwanted and unloved. She talked a lot to hide her insecurities and openly spoke of suicide. She accused me of lying when I used my imagination to tell stories. I did not stop imagining, I stopped telling her stories. She spanked me for wanting candy in a movie so I decided that wanting was bad.

My father was uninvolved in our daily lives. He travelled for a living and was not home often. It seemed to me that he did what he wanted without considering the rest of us. He was moody and never said very much. When he was home mother made sure we behaved. I have few memories of him. I was afraid of making my parents sad or angry. My oldest sister adored me and my other sister - not so much. My oldest sister left for college when I was eight and we moved from Montana to Texas.

My father's job moved us often. I lived in four states and six houses before I was ten years old. I remember no joy at home and always being the *new student* at school was awful. We had no extended family, few meaningful possessions, few friends and the awareness that we would be moving again soon. My family lived in turmoil. I was four when I decided that I needed to take care of them.

I yearned for happiness and set out to make things better. I was smart and wanted to fix what was making me so unhappy. I determined that my thoughts and feelings were bad and they were causing the pain. I became angry with myself for not being able to change my emotions to happy thoughts. In an effort to stop them

I closed down and could not admit how much I was hurting. I stayed helpful and kind around people and pretended I was just fine. No one noticed my pretense and I felt worse.

My father became alcoholic and emotionally abusive, and my mother relied on me for emotional support. I felt sad when she was sad and I cried when she cried. I was terrified of making *us* mad or sad. Her love was conditional on my behavior and I learned to behave as expected, regardless of my own wants or needs. There was uncomfortable tension when I tried to express myself. Because I gave away my power, I had no experience with knowing my own thoughts and feelings. I was unable to set goals, make decisions or dream dreams.

I started high school not knowing anyone. I made a few friends and did a few activities. I acted happy around people but did not quite fit in. College was much the same until a classmate asked me to go flying with him. That beautiful spring afternoon we flew over the state capital, the lakes, and the UT (University of Texas) campus. I was happy. He offered to teach me how to fly. We became friends. I fell in love with flying and he fell in love with me.

Like me, his family dynamics made setting personal goals difficult. He was the only son in a relatively wealthy Jewish family. They did not approve of his leaving an Ivy League school in Boston or his choice of studies, his flying or of his close relationship with me. Ready to assert his independence, he declared that we were going to get married. When I accepted his proposal, my mother told me, "You could do worse." She decided that I had chosen him over her. I am not sure I did not.

I quickly went about earning my place in his large family. I converted to Judaism and did my best to meet everyone's expectations. I was determined to belong but I was aware that I never would. We had three children, a beautiful home and all the trappings of a perfect life. However, I was overwhelmed by the lifestyle and community commitments. I faked happiness and could not admit to my loneliness and unhappiness. My body and mind did my talking. Large patches of my hair fell out and I had chronic fatigue. In the mid-eighties my husband disapproved when I started going to a holistic doctor who used muscle testing, acupuncture, cranial sacral work and other things too weird to be acceptable. My body began to heal, but my self-loathing and inability to enjoy this *perfect life* tormented me. My husband suggested a "shrink" to fix me.

After years of weekly therapy sessions, lots of classes, personal growth workshops and hundreds of self-help books, I knew I had to make changes, but I believed that other people would suffer if I gave my own needs priority. I simply could not live with myself if I did that. I learned much later that the books I found most helpful were based on the teachings from A Course in Miracles[1].

My pain was worse than my fear and I stopped giving my power away and began setting boundaries and making my own decisions. I was happier, but the marriage dissolved. I was heartbroken, shattered, and relieved.

It was hard to adjust from who I had been to who I was. I was not prepared to be a single mother of a daughter with Down syndrome, a defiant eleven-year-old son and a teenage daughter who turned her resentment and anger inward. I had no long-term goals or vision for myself and I felt that I had no choice but to make my children's needs my priority. I was too proud to accept help and too afraid to show vulnerability. I pretended we were just fine.

I have to admit that I played the victim role fairly well. I felt inadequate and misunderstood. I opted out in the familiar way. My body and mind quit. I was diagnosed with bi-polar disorder. Although never hospitalized, I was over medicated and nonfunctional. I lost my job. My daughter moved to a residential home because her father decided I could not take care of her. The diagnosis led me to believe that I was broken and unfit, I had nothing more to lose. I saw no way out of the mess that my thoughts and feelings had created.

From the absolute bottom, I found a solid foundation to push back toward the top. Slowly, I recovered. I had freedom that I had never expected. I began to create a new personality and identity. I spent time drawing bright colorful abstract art that still gives me pleasure. I started to understand that it was not selfish to take care of myself. I rekindled my wonder of nature, took long walks, and spent time around animals. I asked for help from my sisters and got it. Finally, my yearnings to be near my children were stronger than my fears. I packed my possessions and moved for the twenty-second time almost 2,000 miles away.

"When I let go of what I am, then I become what I might be." Lao Tzu

My unlearning took a giant leap when two women came looking for space for their organization to meet. My first ACT gathering felt like a homecoming. It was as if they were saying, "We've been waiting for you." I had never been to a meeting like this and I kept coming back. They created sacred space with the resonance of a crystal bowl for a circle of heart-centered learners open to hearing cutting edge diverse topics from outstanding speakers. New age musicians added a delightful dimension. There was laughter and fun all ending in a gratitude circle. I felt their energy and I was home.

How amazed I was to be recognized and to really be seen. I was astonished that I allowed strangers to see my tears of fear and sadness. They offered insights and healing sessions and I willingly accepted. They empowered me to recognize there was a way past my prior survival tactics and they offered skills and tools. The most powerful tool was my first Reiki attunement.

After a few years of expansion, growth, and thoroughly enjoying monthly gatherings, I wanted to help. I was sent a lengthy *discernment process* to complete before I could join the CCC (Co Creation Council). Intention setting, discernment, consensus and respect were not terms I learned in business school. I was skeptical and intrigued. I discerned that I wanted to know more.

I was astonished that the first principle of the CCC was, "How we are together is more important than what we do." Decisions made by consensus are possible. With the respect, appreciation, support and love I received from the CCC I learned self-love. I learned that things do not happen *to* me, they happen *for* me. I was able to untangle and let go of beliefs and patterns that no longer served me.

With this awareness, I learned to set boundaries, and stopped having to be the fixer of everything. I no longer need to earn my place in the world. I no longer judge myself harshly and I allow myself to have wants and needs. I am aware that I am powerful enough to be gentle.

My beliefs fell away quickly at the realization that what I feared was my own power. Now I increasingly stand in my power. As a Reiki Master and a Shamanic practitioner, I have come to accept that I am a healer with inner strength, intuitive confidence and the spiritual help to accomplish anything. I own my emotions and know that I am powerful and I am considerate; I am a leader and I am a servant; I am a teacher and I am a student, and it is okay to be all of these at the same time.

I do not have to forgive myself for my choices and behavior because I know that I am where I am today because of them. I live in gratitude and now my goal is to be a loving healing presence. My realization is that I have always been a loving healing presence. Therefore, it is not a transformation so much as a homecoming.

As I begin to question my beliefs, I am aware that the belief that I am one, alone and afraid, is gone. I have also questioned the belief of our interconnectedness. The spirit world, animals, the angelic realm, the rocks, crystals, trees, plants, and elementals are all a vital part of me. We all gain insight and guidance from all of their wisdom. The energetic flow is everywhere and everything. We are the same spirit and our breath takes us there. Now I believe in All-One-Ness.

I share my awakening and awareness of unlimited possibilities in the hopes that you will be motivated and inspired to take these steps for yourself and the communities in your circle of influence. It came to me as I wrote, if you change the *i* in illness with *we*, you get *wellness*. Nothing is impossible for a loving group of individuals who share intentions. The world will be better when we each wake up and know these as truths.

Karen Brachman

Karen Brachman is a powerful helper who finds joy in being of service to spirit. She worked hard *doing* but now just wants to *be* a loving presence. She is a Reiki Master, a Shaman, a QiGong student, an artist and an animal lover. Her three adult children taught her how to live from her heart, appreciate special needs, to receive and give unconditional acceptance and love, and enjoy the synchronicities each day. Her curiosity leads to adventures and laughter.

Notes

1. A Course in Miracles, A Foundation for Inner Peace, ISBN: 9606388-9-X

Chapter 14

Imagine – From I to We

—Helen Dierker

Imagine an inner frontier, as boundaryless as space. A vast, dark, starry place that begs us, no ... demands us, to explore because it is a big part of why we are here. The exploration of our Inner Space is exciting, frightening, beautiful, messy, complicated, vague, but also crystal clear, uncomfortable, and ultimately rewarding and the most fulfilling journey of my/our lifetime. It is the exploration of our psyche and the discovery of the Divine Witness, that soft still voice and the soft candle light that illuminates the dark recesses of our mind and heart, the Observer observing the Observer. The solo journey desires to join with others on the same trip as we circle our sun, year after year. We are a complicated endless layer of discovery, sometimes revealing things we must own and change, and other times revealing a new gift we forgot or never knew we had. We will never get to the end of this journey until we exit this planet, and who knows where it goes beyond this lifetime?

Clarity is often found only in the fog. It is the difficulties, losses and traumas of life that often break us open and force us to put one foot in front of the other, as we struggle for reasons and meaning. It forces us to escape the monkey mind, step out of auto pilot and put down the To Do list. It can bring us to our knees as we cry in pain for answers. It is the Dark Night of the Soul. It is the extremely uncomfortable place that forces us to go beyond our edges into the unknown.

It is hard to find the Divine Witness in the hustle and bustle of daily life, but with this power nothing is impossible. Often, we have to sit with ourselves in the darkness until the soft light and still voice makes itself known to us. Yes, it is me and it is you, it is the real Us. The Observer observing the Observer. The Spirit and Soul in each of us is peaceful and wise and, in spite of all our humanness, will love us. We also learn after becoming familiar with our divinity, to love and forgive ourselves for our faults and transgressions; and we must learn to love and forgive others' faults and transgressions.

This is the place that slowly reveals that although we experience this life as an individual, we are really a piece of a magnificent whole. We each bring our own gifts, our own light and value. In this place the walls disappear as they do when we walk on a beautiful day, and take in the beauty of a sun-speckled forest floor and breathe in the scent of pine. It is transformative. In that moment there is no time, no personality, no judgment: only love and awe. It is an opening for the concept of Circular Leadership!

Why play small when in truth we should claim our greatness? Why do you think you were born? I don't think it was ever intended that we take this journey alone.

Imagine taking your Higher Self into a group of individuals that are fellow travelers on the path of Light. I have found such a group in ACT, A Community of Transformation. One purpose of this group is to bring the individual into Circular Leadership and share the Light with all. From a place of Awareness, we seek to bring a myriad of different avenues to support as many as possible in the search for their place and path, like the pieces of a kaleidoscope seeking to add beauty to the whole.

The planet has never needed the shared transformative leadership more than it does now. We are on the edge of a major paradigm shift. The old system is reluctant to let go and the new one coming needs Divine Spirit to preserve life, liberty and justice. In order to do this, we will do better to keep the individual ego in check, build on constructive agreement and/or disagreement, recognize unhealthy competition as divisive, and respect the gifts and talents of each in the circle. It is not easy because our humanness and ego will rear its head sometimes. In those moments I like to think about what the Founder of ACT, Linda Roebuck, told me when I joined the circle: "We love each other into wholeness," and I have witnessed this in this group! I hope it will be the protocol for many more such organizations that are coming to answer the call.

I share this poem because it is a result of my own transformation.

Home
by Helen Dierker

My House stands Alone,
In a neighborhood with many Houses.
And yet I see open fields, teaming with Nature.
My neighborhood is gated, but it is not.

My windows are open wide and the curtains billow
    in my room.
I see, hear, smell, taste and feel Life rushing into
    my space.
Neighbors smiling and talking over the fence,
    children playing, babies,
Dogs and cats, bunnies and a fox – a car screeches
    to a stop. But it's too late!

I see guns and terror; I see knives and blood,
I see a woman battered, her purse stolen.
I see yelling, crying, cheating, lying and pain and misery.
Confused youth and hungry aged!
The privileged and the castaways!
My Heart is Heavy, I am Sad and Angry at the
Injustice!

I walk past my Parlor. I am my Parlor, and the noise
is overwhelming!
Many conversations competing to be heard.
Some are laughing, others irate and arguing.
Some bring good news, others division and hate.

I don't go in, I keep walking down the long dark
corridor.
At the farthest reaches, I come to a door.
Opening the door, is a beautiful, single candle that
brings soft light to the entire room.
The most brilliant light I have ever seen!
I AM invited to sit and rest my weary body with its
confusion, worry, anger and fear – in the softest,
most comfortable chair I ever sat in.

I am alone, but I am not alone. It is like I am at the
most beautiful, expensive restaurant anywhere.
Crystal and china shimmer in the candle light.
I have found "the One", the Love of my life.
I am Elated and so in Love!

We are talking about such interesting matters.
Sweet music plays in the background.
Fear, dread and worry are gone.
I am filled with such Joy, like I never experienced
    before.
Then the small, brilliant candle speaks.
It is the small still voice foretold by the great Prophets.
The Great "I Am", "The Father and I are One."
No words are really necessary –
I know I am Home and this is the real Me.

So, who am I? Who are you?
A Personality, a name, your job, a parent, a status,
A winner or a loser, prestigious or ordinary, rich
    or poor?
With each answer you will find it is Not the truth
    of who you are,
It is layers we wrap around our Ego identity.

Observers to varying degrees,
Watching or participating in Life, telling our stories.
Gathering information, seeking answers, making
    sense of it all.
We are many, many divine spirits, on even more
    missions.

Often looking outside taking it in,
Joining the Parlor talk.

Then sometimes walking down the dark hall,
To the miraculous candle and soft still voice of
wisdom,
To the Great Room with shining crystal and china,
Returning to the Love of the One we have always
been looking for!

Cheers! That is who I am, You are, and We are –
Really!
Perfect fits in the puzzle of Life, each bringing our
own gifts.
Divine Sparks of Eternal Light and Love.
Our Journey is always about returning Home!

Helen Dierker

Helen Dierker is a retired business owner and executive. In college and business her interest was in the individual and providing training and development to her staff and her clients. As President of Neptune Specialty Training, she provided training and Continuing Education credits for insurance agents along the East Coast. Helen has traveled to China to study Eastern Religions and Qigong with Masters. She is a Certified Life Coach and lifelong student of Metaphysics and Spirituality.

Part V

The Ripple
Effect

*"I alone cannot change the world, but I can cast a stone
across the waters to create many ripples."*
—*Commonly attributed to Mother Teresa*

The previous sections of this book highlight the positive impact that participation in a transformative circle can have on the individuals and the group. When people feel valued, connected, purposeful, and impactful, they carry that vibration with them into other engagements and relationships. They take with them a sense of self-acceptance, gratitude, and love, which they engender in others.

This section focuses on how some of the authors are translating their experience with ACT's Circular Leadership into other areas of their life, and how these types of experiences, big and small, can help change the world we live in every day.

Chapter 15

Finding My Voice

—Linda Althaus

The mountain is high. Climbing it can be long and rough at times. However, amidst the climb lie plateaus that provide time for respite, reflection and recharge: a time for play and a time to be still, a time to go within - to reflect and be grateful, possibly a time to nap, to dream … a time to hear the call to the next adventure.

So, who is called to an adventurous climb to the mountain top? A little girl with a vivid imagination.

I was born an only child to loving parents – parents who wanted to protect me and, in this way, became my voice. They were parents who directed my actions and opinions with the best of intentions. This little girl found that it was best to be quiet and not speak from her true voice.

In the sixties, I grew up in a family of low to moderate income who themselves had never attended college. So, what did the majority of girls in the sixties plan for as a career? We became nurses, teachers or secretaries -- learning by example -- doing as we were told. It was only later that we began to question those beliefs and teachings.

As a teenager I dropped out of speech class in high school after the first day. My life was redirected by one speech class: one uncrossable bump along the path.

Since childhood, I wanted to become a nurse. Perhaps it was a calling that began at the time I learned to filet the fish my father caught in Lake Erie. I dove into dissecting all its scaly parts! So why did med school and becoming a doctor never enter my thoughts? Most likely, for the same reason I dropped the speech class: fear of speaking and revealing my true feelings.

Oh, yeah. What about those stumbling blocks on my path to the mountain top? In retrospect, those rough rocks were stepping stones that allowed me to claim my true voice. But those path blocks included the death of my husband and his parents, from cancer; a mother with Alzheimer's; two young children; and a stepdaughter experiencing her own grief of abandonment and loss. All this, within a short period of time, put me in a tailspin. Upside down - an understatement!

The blocks along the way may toss us so far upside down we may wonder if we will ever be upright again. However, in reality, we are given the opportunity to unlearn much of what we have learned and believed was the truth.

So, what was this finding my voice thing all about, and why so difficult? It came down to trust, to finding that truth within me and letting it out, setting it free. During this journey called Life we are faced with many thoughts, feelings and perceptions that we may not want to express outwardly. We fear being exposed. However, as we change, grow and transform, our inner clarity and our truth become the inner light that allows us to go forth and shine.

Through the process of our conditioning and programming by our parents and culture, so many of us develop a voice within that tells us we are not good enough, smart enough, or articulate enough. It's a nagging voice saying, *"Don't speak. You have nothing to offer. You will be ridiculed and, when you stumble, you may freeze and become an embarrassment."*

All along the mountain climb, the silenced true voice keeps trying to break through the barrier to that *insurmountable* mountain top. *"You are a shining light. You have Love in your heart -- a voice to be heard. Speak your true self, loud and clear.*

Which voice do I choose?

It has been documented that over 70% of our thoughts are negative, often keeping us stuck in survival mode: a place where the majority of humans reside. I lived in a fearful and negative thinking mode when I was going through my challenges. Since then, I have learned that the reason most of us remain in the survival mode is the desire to be in control and feel *safe* – an illusion based in fear. To rise above this thinking required faith and trust on my part and an awareness of why I am here on Earth.

Gaining knowledge of my purpose pushed me on towards the ultimate goal of Unconditional Love – to be Love. When our purpose is Love, challenges become opportunities and obstacles become gifts, both providing for growth along our path. I was becoming aware of what was really going on ... I was open.

During this journey called Life, we are faced with many thoughts, feelings and perceptions that we may not want to express outwardly for fear of being exposed. However, as we grow and transform, our inner clarity and truth provide the inner light that allows us to go forth and be the essence of the Love and Light we are.

So, the mountain climb continues and I reach another plateau. This plateau offers a time for contentment, but it cannot be a time of complacency. As I travel upward, the peak looms on the horizon – beautiful, yet seemingly unattainable. How can I break through the barriers that block my reaching the mountain top? *Idleness will never move me upward.* I continue my climb.

I discovered we are not alone. Our guides, angels, and teachers show up in many forms, as long as we are open to receiving them. In my case, helpers began arriving. Many had fur - fluffy white fur, then short black fur, gray fur and ultimately brown fur. Dogs, cats, even pet rats. They all showed up with a message, a gift and love.

Amazing people, communities and organizations surrounded me, helping me to get back on my path to the mountain top. I registered for a noncredit community college class called *Inner Wisdom, Living from the Inside Out*. The self-discovery I experienced in that course was paramount in my climb to the summit. I began to shift my perceptions and beliefs. (The outstanding instructor of that class is the initiator and compiler of this book that I am so honored to be a voice in.) I enrolled in massage therapy school, and, shortly after, became certified. I opened my own massage practice. Additionally, I went on to complete my Reiki Master training. I started to speak - through touch, as a complement to my voice.

Before continuing, I would like to share my professional learning of holistic health with a brief review of our autonomic nervous system (ANS). This is a little physiology, offering a bit of information on the mechanism of action and response, what you may know as *fight or flight*. The ANS is made up of two branches, the *sympathetic* and the *parasympathetic*. The sympathetic branch includes the fight or flight response, activated when we perceive danger. Conversely, the parasympathetic branch lowers our defenses, therefore returning us to a state of calm. It is comprised of two pathways. One, the ventral vagus, supports a sense of calm and centeredness. The other, known as the dorsal vagus, blocks this life-or-death threat. In essence, the second pathway can shut us down, allowing us to become disconnected where we can withdraw back to perceived safety.

It is in our ventral vagus where we have the ability for change, growth and expansion. This is where we feel open-hearted, engaged and joy-filled. Faith and trust enter, and we begin to rethink, rather than blindly going from one thought or belief to another. We are flipped off autopilot. Again, awareness is the gateway to change. By way of slowing down our thoughts, choosing to be mindful and incorporating methods to achieve this (such as meditation, yoga, time in nature, disconnecting from our devices and numerous other practices), we begin to remember our true selves. We change those neural connections and rewire our brain, bringing forth a positive, balanced sense of wellbeing. Our individual practices are required but a nurturing environment is a huge stepping stone to finding ourselves.

A Community of Transformation, ACT, provided a new plateau where I found a nurturing and educational environment. A place where acceptance, diversity, shared thought, and non-judgment was abundant. It is an environment promoting mind-body-spirit connection, individual and collaborative growth, conducive to peace, safety and the ability to speak comfortably without the fear of ridicule: where love is shared and returned.

So why am I writing about my journey in a book about Circular Leadership? Because when I stepped up to join a circle of leaders, I brought my whole self to the group – the fears, gifts, and willingness to evolve. Finding my voice has been instrumental in helping to uncover my true self. It is about going and growing back into the reality of equality, wholeness, and oneness and we don't do it alone.

For the past five years I have been a member of the governing body of ACT. The individual spokes, or members, came together realizing what each had to offer. Each spoke provided a diverse background, but connected as part of the wheel -- not separate, but as part of a whole. We spiral upward in personal and collective growth, energy, purpose, and harmony. We hold that sacred safe space for expansion.

In Circular Leadership, practiced in ACT, authenticity is paramount. In the circle of the governing body of ACT, we connect, we touch, we share, we listen to each other, we are equal, and we do not dominate. We, as a whole, are the sum of all our parts. We then shine forth that Light to make the change together.

Returning to my personal story, as I trudged up that mountain, tripping and falling, ready to give up

many times, a little voice inside kept saying, "Get up."
I fought with it. I swore at it. I had a few pity parties
of *poor me*. I sang along the way the song dedicated to
my graduating nursing class, *You'll Never Walk Alone*
written by Oscar Hammerstein. I sang it, cried with it,
yelled it, but kept it with me to the top.

Hiking along the way, little by little, I realized that
hidden voice of so many years had become history.
From the summit of that mountain, I could see that
the blocks along the way had been opportunities that
allowed for my growth. With all the responsibilities,
challenges and, of course, play time, it was now time
to speak up. I could no longer hide under a pillow.
No more hiding. No more dropped speech classes. No
more silence.

I found my voice! I know, with a little trepidation,
I can stand in front of that class! No longer do I hide
in the shadows, because I now know when I speak it
is the authentic me not fearing judgment, ridicule, or
rejection. If I freeze or stumble, so be it. I laugh. The
time is here to rise, to shine, to be playful … a time
to share and sparkle on our path. In that circle we
remember we are one. On that mountain top it is time -
time to howl, leap, surrender, and let go - transforming
individually and collectively for the next adventure
together.

Linda Althaus

Linda Althaus continues an active life after a nursing career in fields of oncology, home care and hospice. Currently she is treasurer for ACT and on the CCC. Linda is a Reiki Master and also serves as a prayer chaplain at Unity by the Bay Spiritual Center in Annapolis. She has served those in transition by holding a sacred, compassionate environment for them and their families. You may find her traveling cross country, with her rescue pups in her camper, loving a simple life with nature and adventure.

Chapter 16

Successful Belonging: The Energy behind a Genuine Culture of Diversity

—*Kim Watson*

I have a degree in Mathematics. I have over thirty years working in cyber security and its predecessor fields. I am a female who has spent over half her life excelling in male-dominated arenas, and everything I believed about who I am as a role model was recently challenged.

I have a few quotes that I use to guide my behavior. One of my favorites is, "Be the change that you wish to see in the world," usually attributed to Gandhi. For me, this quote is about continually demonstrating the values, dynamics, and results that I would like to see prevalent in the world – and so I thought I was being a great role model for all the young women working for and with me, just by excelling at my job and having access to any and all opportunities that I desired. By completely ignoring gender, I thought I was demonstrating that it was irrelevant ... by being successful inside the existing culture, I thought I was demonstrating that gender was not a limiting characteristic.

A recent conversation with a visionary in my field has made me rethink my position and my behavior. The conversation was focused on diversity in the cyber security workforce: the need to bring together different experiences, talents, and perspectives to radically innovate and solve a seemingly intractable problem. But instead of focusing on who to hire and how to define the blueprint for a diverse workforce, he placed the focus on culture.

We have a significant workforce shortage problem in cyber security, and most experts believe it is only getting worse. So the idea this visionary had was to focus on inclusivity and the culture of your organization. His point, which I had never thought about before, was that if you do not have a culture that honors diversity, then large portions of the eligible workforce will not want to work for you. *You don't hire a culture of diversity, you build and nourish it.*

Looking back, I saw that I had done nothing to change a culture that limited the participation of good people with amazing talents and expertise. My apathy allowed an environment to exist that prevented contributions from, and recognition of, individuals and ideas that might have made significant impact on the state of cyber security.

So, I have decided to change my behavior. I still don't like focusing on differences and investing my energy on the problem, so I need to be the change I want to see ... but what exactly is that change? Clearly it would show that a female can be successful in a profession considered to be dominated by males. Actually, it would show that someone embodying any dimension of diversity could be successful in this profession. It would also include demonstrating how an environment of inclusivity and diversity not only can solve seemingly intractable problems, but might be our only hope in making radical advances in cyber security.

While these outcomes are fairly obvious and even well defined, what it means to embody those changes is not obvious at all. I have spent a fair amount of time in meditation and discernment, trying to identify the energy or intention I need to bring to every engagement if I want my behavior to be in alignment with my objectives.

Reflecting on the discussion that sparked this change, I identified some key characteristics of the culture being described. Everyone should feel seen, heard, and respected. They should not be pigeonholed based on cultural biases, experience, skill, or previous contribution. On the other hand, I have been a part of environments like this where nothing gets done: where the concept of consensus and hearing all sides actually paralyzes the group.

It seems to me that both sides really matter – that everyone contributes and that the very act of being together results in accomplishments. After a lot of debate, discussion, and meditation, I have come up with the phrase, "Successful Belonging." That a culture of diversity that is able to innovate and solve seemingly intractable problems is one in which every person feels they uniquely contribute to the solution. That every contribution is crafted for that engagement, and everyone is proud of the role they play. That the solution is grander than anything any one of them has envisioned, and that everyone feels they play a key role in the development of that solution.

Now I have a mantra for the culture I want to create, and I am ready to start modeling this new behavior. Except I have no idea how to do that when every small engagement is not always a part of some large endeavor. What does success mean in a routine conversation or a mentoring session? How do I make someone feel like they *belong* or uniquely contribute in an email exchange?

At this point, I was looking around to see if there was a worked example I could build from … and then I remembered my time on the Co-Creation Council (CCC) for A Community of Transformation (ACT). The culture of the CCC was exactly what I was trying to create in my world of cyber security. The CCC had members come and go, but continued to make great strides for the organization. Everyone who participated felt it was an empowering, honoring, and genuine experience.

Reflecting back on my time on the CCC, I recognized the fact that all decisions had been consensus based. Everyone felt that they brought all of who they were to the process, contributing insight based on their unique combination of experiences, skills, and perspectives. What was most interesting was that I do not remember a situation where we had to document a dissenting opinion. There was no agreeing to disagree, and therefore the actions taken from that point forward were always performed from a complete commitment by the group of individuals to the singular shared intention.

There were conflicting viewpoints, but no conflicts. The rules of engagement created a safe space for the differing opinions, and the very nature of the decision-making process ensured that everyone contributed in a positive manner. As a result, once the decision process was completed, everyone saw their unique contribution in the solution defined by the collective.

What made this model of leadership so successful for ACT? How could I incorporate the key tenets into my daily engagements at work? These are the questions I need to answer to be the change I want to see ... to embody the culture I am hoping to see created and sustained.

The first tenet I identified is: *How we are together is more important than what we do.* This statement set the tone for every one of our meetings, and became the default way of doing business. It reminded us that no matter how bad our day was, that we were now among friends. People who cared about us and respected us. It reminded us that the business needed to be done, but that act of working together in a positive and heart-felt way was the result that mattered. That any accomplishment or decision was secondary to the intention from which it was created.

As the council members started to embody this philosophy, it changed the way we greeted each other. It changed the way I felt as soon as I entered the room for the CCC meeting. It made it second nature to listen to each and every member, whether they were telling a story or debating a point of business. People rarely interrupted, and when they did it was to ask for a point of clarity or to acknowledge a particularly poignant statement. It is hard to explain the sense of belonging that this type of environment fosters. You really feel that the group can do anything: that the combination of skills, knowledge, and experiences can be infinitely shuffled until a solution emerges and a plan develops; that your participation as an individual is critical to the success of the whole; that without your unique contributions, the group would be missing a set of talents, expertise, and insight that would limit their options.

The second tenet that seems important is the dedicated commitment to individual transformation and healing. Every person on the CCC was expected to be actively pursuing their own journey of awakening, enlightenment, transformation, etc. They were encouraged to talk about their experiences, their struggles, and their epiphanies.

We engaged in retreats designed to foster individual growth as a way to strengthen and evolve the group.

As individuals continued down their own unique path of healing and transformation, what they brought to the group changed. The group honored and respected both those changes and the new contributions derived from them. No one was trapped in a set of expectations based on past behavior or the roles they had previously played. There was always the opportunity to take a new skill or perspective and immediately apply it to a current situation, discussion, activity, or decision. I believe this is why the turnover on the CCC is as high as it is when everyone who participates considers it one of the most valuable experiences of their lives. They go through profound shifts that attract new opportunities. That is what happened to me. Some members have been on the CCC since its inception, but who they are, the work they do, and the way they participate has changed significantly over the years. It is almost like incorporating new members all the time ... members that do not require any on-boarding because they already know how the council works.

Based on my experiences, derived from the practice of these two tenets, I have decided that the belonging I want to encourage has multiple facets. First, I want people to believe that they are appreciated for all the different skills, experiences, and knowledge that they bring to the project or organization. I want the role they play at any time to be based on the situation, the need, and their passion/interest. I do not want their role to be inherited based on previous failures or successes, no matter how much easier that is, because I expect them to change and grow. Lastly, I want them to feel seen, heard, and appreciated, to feel pride in ownership of team decisions, actions, and outcomes.

As for success, I now realize that this is more about the intention and the practice than the result. I consider the engagement a success for me if the person's sense of belonging increases. I consider it a success for the others if they leave with an improved sense of self-worth that they are willing to share. I want every engagement to inspire the other person to believe that they have more to contribute. That not only is there a group that wants to receive that contribution, but that it will increase the capability of the group to have the impact it desires.

My hope is that I will be creating and nourishing a culture that genuinely embraces and benefits from diversity by changing my behavior to embody the energy/intention of Successful Belonging. I hope that this culture enables people to make great advances against a myriad of seemingly intractable problems. I also hope that these same people have the confidence and support to cultivate experiences that enable them to be more present and participate more fully in their lives.

While this sounds like a dream, it is anchored in reality. I have participated in a group that, in fact, has done all of the above. I have a worked example that has demonstrated that the adherence to a few key tenets, combined with core practices, can sustain a culture that inspires individuals, generates results, improves quality of life, and positively impacts the world. This is what I want to be remembered for – that I made others feel like they belonged and enabled them to be successful beyond their dreams. I have no interest in being remembered as a female who excelled in a male-dominated world.

Kim Watson

Kim Watson is an empath and intuitive who works with multiple healing modalities. In her day job, she is a member of the Senior Staff at the Johns Hopkins Applied Physics Laboratory and is the Technical Director for Integrated Adaptive Cyber Defense (IACD). She has been a member of ACT for over fifteen years and was a member of the CCC from 2003-2007.

Chapter 17

The Alchemy of Manifestation

—Dr. Stephany Porter

I t was a dream come true.
Do you dare to dream? *Truly* dream? How many of your dreams have become reality? It takes imagination to step out of your current reality; and, it takes consciousness to manifest the new reality. In a group environment, when individuals join together with a common focus, the energy exponentially rises to meet the group and their intentions.

In 1993, frustrated with the limitations of conventional medicine in relation to the treatment of a loved one with cancer, our family sought additional options. During this time I discovered the world of natural medicine and became enthusiastic about its benefits to humanity. After acquiring my Doctorate in Naturopathic Medicine (N.D.) I accepted a position in Montana where N.D.s are licensed as physicians with a full scope of practice. In 2006 the desire to live closer to family and friends and to provide naturopathic medicine in my hometown overrode the limitations of practicing in an unlicensed state. Upon returning to Maryland and joining the Maryland Naturopathic Association, a small group of us set the intention to achieve licensure in our state. We succeeded in 2014 when our legislation was passed by the General Assembly. The commitment of a few lead to the manifestation of a dream even when many said it was not possible.

The deeper question of health, healing and what does a world without suffering look like, burned inside me like a forest fire in a drought. Philosophy, spirituality and mysticism provided new directions to explore. At this point I found ACT (A Community of Transformation): a manifestation of Linda. It was an honor, and still is, to be part of this special group. Here, we created a sacred space, where the growth of the individual and community are at the forefront, and the support of the group is the platform.

When we are in community, our minds are stretched, allowing for new possibilities. This energy increases the flow from our conscious to our subconscious, enacting the universal law of attraction, leading to the movement of energy into matter.

Through quantum physics, we have learned that there are infinite possibilities and potential. It is up to us to choose a reality and summon the universe to manifest it. At the point when a person, or the group, makes a choice, no other possibilities exist until that chosen intention is no longer held, or deemed suitable. When that held intention is released, matter is returned back to energy. With intention, focus and discipline, the opportunity to arrive at a decision point is much more likely to occur.

The average person has approximately 30,000 thoughts per day. In a group of eight that is 240,000 per day, or 3,000,000 in a group of one hundred. All of them funnel into the collective subconscious. Our nervous system is the home for these thoughts in the physical form. This electric and magnetic system enables a connection between the universe (now multiverse) and matter (physical form), and is a bridge to understand oneness.

So how, then, does a group consciously manifest in these challenging, interesting and ever-changing times? Are there any limitations?

In the beginning, a group comes together around a problem or issue that individuals cannot find a solution to themselves. They develop a shared vision and a focused intention that outlines their mission and goals. This is what occurred when I joined the small group of Naturopathic doctors seeking to obtain licensure for our profession in Maryland.

Each entity, or sentient being, in a group is a beaming thread of light. As each thread comes together, a small entanglement occurs creating a connection that allows for further reach. As more threads join, their entanglement forms a multi-dimensional mesh, or net, with increased *tensegrity*, a relatively new word formed by combining the words *tension* and *integrity*. (Tensegrity is found in nature and is now being implemented in architecture and other areas to accomplish more with less.)

This multi-dimensional net, or matrix, expands the group's boundaries, allowing for even greater possibilities. With fewer constraints, the group is then free to dream more and go beyond their perceived individual limits.

With limitless boundaries, the group can be in a land of playfulness, where visions are not restricted to this third dimensional reality. The net is strengthened even more with increased input, experience and diversity. The unknown no longer feels scary. It is in this higher vibration that manifestation occurs and can then become grounded here on earth.

"No problem can be solved by the same consciousness that created it." Albert Einstein.

The difference in today's humanity is our conscious understanding of the power of choice. We know that our thoughts create and that we can choose the thoughts we want to hold in our minds or our awareness. The importance of this knowing, understanding, or re-awakening within us, is instrumental in our evolution. There appear to be some rules with regards to how the conscious and subconscious work, or exist, in this current state. Our consciousness, not to be confused with our brain, has free will, while our subconscious does not. What lands in the subconscious is acted upon, irrelevant of discernment, judgment or free will. It is up to each individual to be aware of what they funnel from their conscious to their subconscious, in relation to themselves and the group. As this consciousness builds and works in its highest vibration, using our higher mental faculties, so does the pull on the universe to deliver, or manifest, the vision.

We have invested a great deal in the reductionism model of science, medicine and physics. Our aim has been to identify the components of life, down to the atomic level, in an attempt to explain the whole from the smallest part. We have now found that the whole is greater than the sum of its parts. No single part explains the whole; no constituent of an herb explains the actions of the whole herb; no atom explains how a seed becomes a tree. In other words, a group is far greater than the sum of its parts. Therefore, when a group consciousness persistently works towards a common vision, the possibilities are as endless as your imagination. This is alchemy at its best.

This all takes patience, meditation, group time and the art of listening. It is important to understand that it may not happen in the exact way you expect. It is necessary to stay open and allow your intuition to guide you. Staying in conscious awareness of your vibration (thoughts) is essential. Are you responding from fear, judgment or expectations? Or are you responding from love, light and your inner knowingness? I often check to see if I have my fear goggles on, for I know they cloud my decisions. When I set them down, my ability to discern and become congruent with who I really am increases: i.e. manifesting is easier. Conscious awareness is mandatory and serves to maintain integrity in the individual and, therefore, the group.

Change is hard. You as an individual and as a group must make time for listening, even when your patience is worn thin. When I first joined ACT, I came from a strong business background, having worked with professional boards. ACT challenged my patience. Initially, it appeared that we were moving at a snail's pace and there were not definable, accountable goals achieved at each meeting. Although some structure is beneficial, too much structure strangles the imagination. Over time, I realized this board was different. There was a freedom I felt that lead to a deeper understanding of self. The tensegrity of the group allowed for a natural ability to discern from my inner knowing (intuition).

A stronger individual leads to a stronger group. Strength and vulnerability, in a matrix of love, dissolve fear. Leadership is not leading; it is carving a path, with many new doors, allowing the individual to open the one that suits them, increasing their inner wisdom and strength. The Circular Leadership Model lets each individual step up when their specific skill is needed for the task at hand.

Change is Alchemy: a form of speculative thought, also known as transformation. It is most often associated with turning lead into gold, a cure for a disease, or finding the fountain of youth. New understandings are returning us to the definition found in the Hermetic principle, that our thoughts create and have the ability to move energy into matter or vice versa.

As we learn to harness our mental faculties (imagination, intuition, perception, memory, reason and will), free ourselves of toxic thoughts (judgment, fear, expectations and attachment), and allow the love and light from within to shine through, our vibration will rise to meet the creative potential that we are. My Guru and teacher, Sai Maa, has helped me to understand the importance and breadth of these mental faculties, especially reason (the ability to think properly), because reason is, "the magic in the marriage of matter and energy."

You become your thoughts and your thoughts create. We are constantly transmitting and receiving energy. So be the leader of your life. Be the thread in the matrix that strengthens your group's net, allowing for possibilities beyond your imagination. Consciously choose in each moment and your dreams will come true.

Stephany Porter

Dr. Stephany Porter graduated from Bastyr University in Kenmore, WA. Her passion for integrative oncology led her to seek a degree in Naturopathic medicine and become a FABNO (Fellow of the American Board of Naturopathic Oncology). She founded The Bodhi Clinic and has served on various boards. Her passion for understanding *dis-ease* (being out of ease), has led her to study various spiritual paths and practices. As a student of life, she has had the honor of speaking to professional groups and providing workshops for her clients on topics that range from nutrition, to the effect of herbs on cell signaling, to mastering our minds for our true creative powers. www.BodhiClinic.com.

Chapter 18

Choosing to Evolve to Higher Consciousness ... or not!

—Ed Roebuck aka Sir-Laughs-A-Lot

One of the most intriguing things about life is that, at any moment and through any encounter, we can experience the surprise of an energetic sharing. We share the heart energy connection that knows the truth of each other. We each have the gift of choosing the eyes we look out of and what we see. We can readily shift from judgment to appreciation and honoring. Such gifts we give each other!

As we learn more about the cosmos as a spiraling rising of energy consciousness, we understand that science and spirituality have more in common than we have ever realized. Divine undulating, vibrational energy flows in a timeless way, existing in every moment, with every moment being now. I believe that the seed of A Community of Transformation (ACT) was birthed from this universal energy as a calling. In the mid-nineties, my wife, Linda, began to feel an energetic pull for the creation of a heart-centered mind, body and spirit community. Her spiritual practices, experiences with Reiki and other forms of energy work, led her to a heightened sense of intuition on what she was to do. In this same time period, I also chose to be on a path of raising my holistic and integrated consciousness: from the outside in and the inside out.

After looking for nearly a year, we had found a spiritual community (Unity) that felt right and became actively involved in the leadership that was charged with expansion and growth of consciousness. We were at the center of the planning and implementation of two other organizations: the Beacon of Light Center, and Creative Conversations, Inc. Both were focused on mind-body-spirit connection and higher consciousness and evolution. We immersed ourselves in metaphysics, healing arts, and spiritual study groups that excitingly expanded our knowing of who we are and what we are here to do. We experienced joy in the journey and celebrated our resonance of oneness. I didn't know I was so spiritually hungry. My perceptions of reality shifted to awareness and focused attention of my/our essence and interconnectedness of everything.

This enhanced my awareness of the energetic field, and I felt a deeper knowing of my own essence and an appreciation for my place and purpose in the earth plane. As Linda's intuitive experiences became more connected to the Divine, my experiences with this energetic field also expanded.

Linda and I chose to participate together in these high-vibrational experiences and our connection to universal energy and to each other deepened. My formulation of this upwardly spiraling energy took shape. Together we rise and embrace life in a more meaningful and purposeful way, and experience more peace and joy.

This graphic image of the evolution of ACT is set within the energetic field of the spiraling, creative, ever-expanding energy of our understanding of the universe. It shows how divine undulating energies have flowed throughout time, and how at one unique moment ACT Annapolis sprung (yet another spiral image) forth.

The *calling in* of our collective intentions, coupled with the personal *going within* of the founding members in 2001 gave birth to the Co-Creation Council (CCC). Through time our CCC circle would spin, and this created the cyclical aspect which is represented in the graphic illustration. This vortex of divine energies flowing through us, from outside in and from inside out, inspired us to co-create ACT.

What emerged became the catalyst for the manifestation of a creative space where visionaries could express themselves, the curious could learn, and the seeds of hope could take root in meaningful friendships. Word spread slowly, at first. Yet, as with any idea whose

A spiraling
rising of energy
of consciousness

ACT

CCC

Light

Frequency

Vibration

Energy

An image of the
birthing of ACT

time has come, momentum carried us forward with joy. Attendance at our gatherings increased, regular meetings became monthly, guest speakers and musicians broadened our growth, and we soon had to expand our perception of what was possible.

Today we celebrate how ACT has grown and matured into what we might refer to as "ACT Beyond," as in beyond our initial vision and geographic reach. It's almost as if today, as we are turning 18 years old, our baby has grown up, matured, and needs to move out of the house. Publishing this anthology is a realization of our initial shared visions yet is also the birthing of our current shared intentions.

ACT Annapolis will continue to touch hearts locally and be an expansive vehicle for creativity, healing, and positive transformation. What happens beyond today, however, is in the creative hearts and sacred visions of many others, some of whom are just now reading our story. On the reader's journey this might serve as a map of our path through vibrational, energetic terrain and the alignment of our collective intentions with a higher purpose.

The following poem created itself from my thinking, feeling, and knowing heart. It came upon me in a sudden moment of remembering — a moment of knowing. When it came, it was an incredible feeling of subtle, but profound, awareness of the gifts of my many incredible learning experiences.

Love Come Tricklin' Down
by Ed Roebuck

What is it that strikes at the heart,
    that hits a chord,
    that touches the soul,
Causing us to silently speak, without intent or plan –
    of truth, beauty, joy,
    of love, hurt and pain.
Just for a moment, just in the moment,
    briefly holding back the wordless sounds –
    I speak with a teardrop that has welled up,
    so fast, not asked permission, but has come just
    the same.

I brush it away, as not to be counted,
    and in silent wailing I seek to look cool and
    serene.
But then comes another from within, a heart message
    encased in a tear; has to get out! Can't be denied!
    Lest I choke it off like an un-sneezed sneeze.
It swells up, so full the drop that the eye can't contain;
    so,
    Trickle down joy.
    Trickle down shame.
    Trickle down heart.
    Trickle down pain.
    Trickle down love.

There I am standing naked in the moment.

If I dare look around and see the face of another,
     the face of a sister or brother – wet with tear,
     or filled with smile, for they too have
     had a moment – so we smile, within or
     without, and maybe even touch one another –
Without words we share a moment – of joy,
     of oneness, of peace, of unity.

In a moment there has been "truth revealed," a touch
     to the chord within the heart, within the soul
now gone, fleet-footed into the past.
Left we are with an insight or sense of
     touch, awareness, growth – about what and
     where we are.

Automatically, quickly we move on, maybe
     later to reflect; left with a knowing that somehow,
     somewhere, soon there will be a next time,
     and *Love Will Come Tricklin' Down.*

When there is a pull to respond to the Universe's prompting it is like the phrase, "An idea whose time has come." Then, one has the choice to embrace or ignore, to accept or not.

Linda and I chose to evolve to higher consciousness!

Ed Roebuck
Ed Roebuck is a heart-centered beacon of light and love. He recently retired after 54 years in education as a

teacher, trainer, curriculum specialist and administrator. A friend, a listener and reflector, he is a teacher, both professionally and in the game of life. He loves coaching and working with youth. Ed is a Karuna and Usui Reiki Master. Sir-Laughs-A-Lot likes to play and is an aspiring poet. He loves nature and finding crystals.

Epilogue

The Next Call

If I had not followed Inner Guidance almost two decades ago this book would not have been birthed. The people who have been served by our organization would not have had personal growth experiences that enriched and transformed their lives.

It's about service. Yes, service ... It is high service when you step up to call the circle you are meant to lead. Whether it's your family, a group in the workplace, an organization, a team within an established circle, etc., it starts with you. It begins by getting quiet ... and still... and listening to the soft voice of your intuitive heart.

A circle represents wholeness. You are a circle. I am a circle. As we become leaders of our own individual circle and join with others in love we begin to wake up together. Humanity's consciousness is raised and the world is changed ... for real! That's what Circular

Leadership is about.

Are you ready to do your part to change the world -- to do the things that only you were preordained to do? Listen to the call of your heart. Answer the call. Make the call.

Will you make the call?

Together we rise, together we thrive.
We believe in circles because circles take no sides.
Together we win, when everyone is in,
When every little hand and every little heart
Touches every little piece and every little part.

Appendix 1

Vision and Mission

A Community of Transformation (ACT)
www.actannapolis.org

ACT is a nonprofit educational organization dedicated to transformation in individuals, communities and the Earth. We integrate mind, body and spirit to achieve peace, harmony, wholeness, and wisdom.

Our Vision
We are an inspirational, heart-centered community that nurtures profound transformation.

Our Mission
Society is undergoing a fundamental transformation in the way it views the world and our role in it. A new

world view is unfolding and it is our goal to assist individuals as they open to this new reality, shifting from a material and limited world, to an interconnected world of relationships, rich in meaning, and alive with consciousness and spirit.

This evolving scientific understanding of the Universe encompasses the potentials and powers of consciousness, including: perceptions, beliefs, attention, intention, and intuition. These new understandings give us a solid framework for creating our lives and playing an active role in attracting what we want. This framework also underscores our significant role in creating the future of the planet and, ultimately, the universe.

Appendix 2

History

ACenter of Transformation was envisioned, in 2001, in response to a desire of a small group of individuals, to offer an array of holistic health services in the greater Annapolis area. This vision was of a facility or campus-like environment to provide services of education, holistic health and related research.

A Center of Transformation (ACT) was incorporated in Maryland in 2001 as a 501(c)(3) nonprofit, educational, membership-organization, focused on holistic health. The name was legally changed to A Community of Transformation in 2007 to better reflect that we were operating more as a community rather than providing services within a facility.

Early on, ACT sponsored two major conferences and one major event in collaboration with the local community college. Internationally known presenters have included Peter Russell, Dr. Christine Page, Dr. James Gordon, Dr. Joe Dispenza, James Twyman, Flo Aeveia Magdalena, and Katye Anna Clark. Through the intimate work some of these people undertook with the governing board, the twelve-member Co-Creation Council has become a cohesive force and the entire organization has expanded and evolved to new levels of operation and consciousness.

Some of these worked intimately with our governing board, the Co-Creation Council, to evolve.

ACT operates with all volunteers in sponsoring ongoing monthly gatherings with speakers and musicians, offering education, inspiration, interaction, and exploration. Sixty to a hundred people attend the gatherings, which focus on energy awareness, individual and collective consciousness-raising, personal development, and understanding the connection between science and spirituality.

ACT has continued to sponsor book study groups and co-sponsors events that are in alignment with ACT's purpose, such as workshops, salons, retreats and Reiki shares. Two celebrations are offered to the community annually, giving opportunity to network and play. Following our vision and mission, ACT determined that *how* we are together is more important than *what* we do.

Appendix 3

Governance and Process

The Co-Creation Council (CCC), a twelve-member governing board, continues to operate with Circular Leadership. Prospective members of the Council use a self-discernment process in applying to serve on the Council. In turn, the CCC approves new members using consensus. A smaller team, comprised of the Chair, Associate Chair, Scribe, Treasurer, and Program Coordinator, meets in between regularly-scheduled monthly board meetings.

Discernment and Decision-Making (more info in Chapter 9)

For ACT, the discernment process is used on a continuing basis to address specific questions and issues related to planning and operations. The process is used to unfold new ideas, to clarify direction, to make decisions, and to inspire action.

In consensus, each person can paraphrase the issue and can live with a particular decision for the good of the group. This process may not bring unanimity, but it creates a decision that everyone can adopt until revisited.

Appendix 4

Lotus Symbol

The Lotus is the adopted symbol for ACT. The concept developed organically in the early stages of the organization and represents the calling in of our collective intentions: Light, Order, Truth, Union and Spirit; or as an acronym, L.O.T.U.S. The following song was written by Mahri Best, a beloved, talented and creative member of ACT who served on the board for two years. We honor her life and appreciate her contributions.

The Lotus Connection
By Mahri Best

We are light that is love without condition,
We are order in our heart and in our mind.
We are truth –we are union and we always will
  believe
We are spirits in this sacred space we find.

We are love that supports all understanding,
We learn—we teach—we heal — we share our gift.
We are like the lotus flower unfolding,
We are dedicated to create world shift.

We are peace and love and joy – we are one—
We're the lotus flowers unfolding in the sun.
We work tirelessly until our work is done
In the blending of our souls we are one.
We are one.

Francie Boyce

Vicki Fearey

J. Arthur

Richard Bredeson

Rev. Rosemary Bredeson

Stephanie Sera

Ed Roebuck

Gloria Hesseloff

Carol Ann Robbins, PhD

Stephany Porter, ND

Linda Roebuck

Linda Althaus

Bob Sima

Marilyn Apirian

Kim Watson

Shannon Marie Plummer

Karen Brachman

Lillia Shoshanna Rae

Helen Dierker

About Linda Roebuck

L inda Roebuck touches hearts and empowers others to be more than they ever imagined they could be. This is her service.

Linda's early career path set the foundation for her current transformational mission. She began as an elementary school teacher and later taught middle and high school students. She earned a Masters degree in Counseling Psychology and moved into guidance counseling and instructional leadership training. This ultimately led to leadership positions at the Maryland State Department of Education. Her success as the leader of a collaborative public-private statewide interagency training program led to her being designated the Department's Interagency Coordinator.

After more than twenty-five gratifying years of public service, Linda felt a strong yearning to fulfill a greater purpose in life ... so strong, that the fear of stepping beyond the structure of bureaucracy became insignificant. She took a six-week sabbatical for personal growth and self reflection that evolved into early retirement.

By following Inner Guidance, Linda began to experience a peaceful connectedness to a knowing that something better was ahead. As part of that knowing, Linda was given a compelling vision of a Holistic Healing Center. The vision persisted until she made a clear commitment to take action. Linda invited interested parties in the local community to participate in a general meeting. The overwhelming response resulted in a creative flow that gained its own momentum and others were soon drawn to join in. Dream teams were created and monthly planning meetings evolved into the organization of A Community of Transformation (ACT).

If Linda had not followed her Inner Guidance almost two decades ago this book would not have been birthed. Her willingness and determination to pursue her passion awakened a community to a journey of personal growth and transformation. Each story in this book is a testament to that journey.

As we become leaders of our own individual circle and join with others in love we begin to wake up together. Humanity's consciousness is raised and the world is changed ... for real! That's what Circular Leadership is all about.

Acknowledgements

My heart is filled with deep gratitude for the many people who helped bring this anthology into reality. I'd like to begin by thanking my awesome Transformational Author Coach, Christine Kloser, for supporting my decision to shift mid-stream from publishing my memoir to this multi-authored anthology and for being with me every step of the way.

To Carrie Jareed whose guidance, organizational skills and helpful structures made going through the publishing process more like a cake walk than work. And, to the entire Capucia Publishing Team, especially Jean Merrill, I say thank you!

To Simon Whaley, editor extraordinaire, who accepted the task of reviewing and editing nineteen different writing styles. You certainly rose to the challenge!

To Gail McClain, our amazing Graphic Designer, who took my visual concepts and turned one into a beautiful book cover that carries the message of connected circles spiraling together and the other into the graphic

CIRCULAR LEADERSHIP

which appears in Chapter 18. I am in awe and appreciation of your skill and commitment to excellence.

To my co-authors – what can I say about how wonderful it has been to be on the journey with you over the past months! Each of you stepped up, some with trepidation about writing, to meet our submission timelines. Thank you for your imaginative creativity and perseverance. We are now poised for an extended journey together as we take our message out into the world.

I would be remiss if I did not call out Kim Watson, who spent two days helping to develop the organizational structure of our book; Lilia Shoshanna Rae, who read every word with me as we prepared to send our first drafts; Karen Brachman, who spent countless hours helping with proof reading and technical requirements in preparing the manuscript; J. Arthur, who was always available to assist when one experienced writer's block or needed clarity; Vicki Fearey, who dropped whatever she was doing to help with suggestions when I was stuck; Francie Boyce, who spent hours reading and reviewing the manuscript; and, Richard Bredeson, webmaster and technical guru, who could always be counted on to fix glitches or offer guidance. The commitment each of you made to this project is commendable and I am forever grateful.

To consultants Peter Russell, Flo Magdalena, Christine Page, M.D., and Teresa Shattuck, thank you for working with our Co-Creation Council at various times throughout the past eighteen years. Your knowledge, wisdom, recommendations and guidance have been incorporated into our processes and have contributed to the ongoing success of our organization.

To my two sons, Ted Jones and Aaron Roebuck, and their families – I am eternally grateful for your love, support and patience as I have been working on this project.

And finally, to my husband Ed, my Soul Partner and supporter, I offer my deepest gratitude for your constant encouragement, willingness to proofread, edit, and for your incredible ability to put up with me at times when I was under pressure. You are the Love of my Life and, as you know, Together We Rise!

Made in the USA
Middletown, DE
31 October 2019